CANARY BREEDING
FOR
BEGINNERS

A PRACTICAL, UP-TO-DATE GUIDE TO THE CULT
OF CANARY BREEDING, DESIGNED SPECIALLY
FOR
THE USE OF THE BEGINNER IN THE HOBBY.

BY

CLAUDE ST. JOHN.

British Library Cataloguing-in-Publication Data
A catalogue record for this book is available from the
British Library

CONTENTS

Aviculture

'Aviculture' is the practice of keeping and breeding birds, as well as the culture that forms around it, and there are various reasons why people get involved in Aviculture. Some people breed birds to preserve a specific species, usually due to habitat destruction, and some people breed birds (especially parrots) as companions, and yet others do this to make a profit. Aviculture encourages conservation, provides education about avian species, provides companion birds for the public, and includes research on avian behaviour. It is thus a highly important and enjoyable past time. There are avicultural societies throughout the world, but generally in Europe, Australia and the United States, where people tend to be more prosperous, having more leisure time to invest. The first avicultural society in Australia was The Avicultural Society of South Australia, founded in 1928. It is now promoted with the name Bird Keeping in Australia. The two major national avicultural societies in the United States are the American Federation of Aviculture and the Avicultural Society of America, founded in 1927. In the UK, the Avicultural Society was formed in 1894 and the Foreign Bird League in 1932. The Budgerigar Society was formed in 1925.

Some of the most popular domestically kept birds are finches and canaries. 'Finches' are actually a broader category, encompassing canaries, and make fantastic domestic birds, capable of living long and healthy lives if given the requisite care. Most species are very easy to breed, and usefully do not grow too large (unlike their larger compatriot the budgerigar), and so do not need a massive living space. 'Canary' (associated with the *Serinus canaria*), is a song bird is native to the Canary Islands, Madeira, and the Azores – and has long been kept as a cage bird in Europe, beginning in the 1470s. It now enjoys an international following, and the terms *canariculture* and *canaricultura* have been used in French, Spanish and Italian respectively, to describe the keeping and breeding of canaries. It is only gradually however (a testament to its growing popularity) that English breeders are beginning to use such terms. Canaries are now the most popular form of finch kept in Britain and are often found still fulfilling their historic role of protecting underground miners. Canaries like budgies, are seed eaters, which need to dehusk the seed before feeding on the kernel. However, unlike budgerigars, canaries are perchers. The average life span of a canary is five years, although they have been known to live twice as long.

Parakeets or 'Budgies' (a type of parrot) are another incredibly popular breed of domestic bird, and are originally from Australia, first brought to Europe in the 1840s. Whilst they are naturally green with yellow heads and black bars on the wings in the wild, domesticated budgies come in a massive variety of colours. They have the toes and beak typical of parrot like birds, as in nature they are climbers; budgies are hardy seed eaters and their strong beak is utilised for dehusking seeds as well as a climbing aid. When kept indoors however, it is important to supplement their diet of seeds with fresh fruit and vegetables, which would be found in the wild. Budgies are social birds, so it is most important to make sure they have company, preferably of their own kind. They do enjoy human companionship though, and may be persuaded, if gently stroked on the chest feathers to perch on one's finger. If not kept in an aviary, they need a daily period of free flight, but great care must be taken not to let them escape.

Last, but most definitely not least, perhaps the most popular breed of domestic bird, is the 'companion parrot' – a general term used for *any* parrot kept as a pet that interacts with its human counterpart. Generally, most species of parrot can make good companions. Common domestic parrots include large birds such as Amazons, African Greys, Cockatoos, Eclectus, Hawk-headed Parrots and Macaws; mid-sized birds such as Caiques, Conures, Quakers, Pionus, Poicephalus, Rose-Ringed parakeets and Rosellas, and many of the smaller types including Budgies, Cockatiels,

Parakeets, lovebirds, Parrotlets and Lineolated Parakeets. The *Convention on International Trade in Endangered Species of Wild Fauna and Flora* (also known as CITES) has made the trapping and trade of all wild parrots illegal, because taking parrots from the wild has endangered or reduced some of the rarer or more valuable species. However, many parrot species are still common; and some abundant parrot species may still be legally killed as crop pests in their native countries. Endangered parrot species are better suited to conservation breeding programs than as companions.

Parrots can be very rewarding pets to the right owners, due to their intelligence and desire to interact with people. Many parrots are very affectionate, even cuddly with trusted people, and require a lot of attention from their owners. Some species have a tendency to bond to one or two people, and dislike strangers, unless they are regularly and consistently handled by different people. Properly socialized parrots can be friendly, outgoing and confident companions. Most pet parrots take readily to trick training as well, which can help deflect their energy and correct many behavioural problems. Some owners successfully use well behaved parrots as therapy animals. In fact, many have even trained their parrots to wear parrot harnesses (most easily accomplished with young birds) so that they can be taken to enjoy themselves outdoors in a relatively safe manner without the risk of flying away.

Parrots are prey animals and even the tamest pet may fly off if spooked. Given the right care and attention, keeping birds is usually problem free. It is hoped that the reader enjoys this book.

FOREWORD

In this series of articles it will be my aim and object to instruct the veriest tyro how to successfully breed a Canary, and to give him a general knowledge of and insight into all the appliances and requirements for carrying on the hobby—in short, I propose to start at the seed-germ, as it were, of Canary breeding, and adhere to its first principles all through, so that even the reader, who, at present, may be utterly unconscious even of the existence of any varieties or breeds in the kingdom of Canarydom, may be able to follow the instructions through the season, step by step, and find himself at the close in the proud position of possessing a few youngsters of his own raising, and, what is far more important, equipped with a sufficient stock of knowledge to start afresh next season with a better class of bird. Thus the tyro of to-day may be the amateur of next season, and by gradual progress fairly hope to take his place among the ranks of successful breeders a few seasons hence.

This being our professed aim, I cannot but claim the indulgence of the already accomplished breeder when he finds me entering into detail and describing what may appear to him the most trivial and obvious matters. Doubtless there was once a time when he himself was puzzled to know what such terms as "egg-drawers" and "nest-pans" meant, and it is to help the would-be fancier who is in a like condition to-day that my efforts are directed. With these few words of preface I proceed at once with my task.

In the vast majority of cases the first thought of embarking in the hobby of Canary breeding arises out of the possession of a single pet song bird. Or, it may be, as we have known in some cases, that a so-called songster never does sing, for the very good reason that it proves to be a hen, when the owner upon discovering the state of affairs is prone to think—Well, if it will not sing, it might at least breed. And so he determines to get a mate for it and try his skill in that direction. It is then the making of a new fancier commences.

Having arrived at this determination he should go to work and lay all his plans methodically. Naturally, in so doing, the first consideration that arises is as to where and how the breeding operations are to be carried on—whether by pairing up the birds in cages, or by allowing them to fly loose in a spare room. As a general rule, I would not advise the beginner to adopt the latter course, because it is practically impossible to breed good exhibition birds under such conditions. It is, therefore, far better that the beginner who aspires to breed good stock in the future should serve his apprenticeship, so to speak, by mastering the art of breeding Canaries in cages, for although the fancier who succeeds in the breeding of caged-up birds is almost certain to succeed with groups flying in comparative freedom, it by no means follows that the reverse holds equally good.

CHAPTER I

THE CAGES CONSIDERED.

I will consider first the case of the fancier who may be going to start with one or two pairs, and has not the luxury of a spare room of any kind to devote to the needs of his hobby. His first requirement will be suitable breeding cages—one cage of the single or double pattern being required for each pair of birds. Within certain limits the choice of breeding cages may be left to the breeder, and a handy man with very few and primitive tools can make very serviceable cages with the aid of the removable wire fronts which are sold nearly everywhere, and largely advertised in the columns of *Cage Birds*. These wire fronts, which are made to any required size, and are arranged so that they slip in the front of the cage, to be taken out again at pleasure, are in reality the complete wire-work (including doors) of the cage. They are constructed on a framework of flat, tinned bars, punched with holes to take the wires, which are afterwards soldered in position. With a "Tate" sugar box or a "Quaker Oat" box (from the grocer), these fronts permit of suitable and very cheap cages being constructed.

But whatever style of cage is adopted, the essential feature that should never be departed from by a hair's-breadth is good workmanship, so that no ragged or rough edges of wood be left about the cage, and no open joints or badly-fitting angles are to be found. Good sound materials must also be demanded to guard against warping and opening of joints, and splitting of boards. All these little accidents, though extremely trivial in themselves, are apt to store up trouble for the breeder in the future, affording, as they do, lodgment for dirt and disease germs, as well as being enticing harbours for red mite—one of the worst foes the breeder may have to contend against.

The one great object should be to secure a perfectly even smooth surface all over the cages, inside and out, so that neither dirt nor insect pests can ever find a hiding place about them. It will at once become apparent that with these essential features in view the cages cannot be made too simply and plainly, and that ornamentation of any and every kind should be strictly avoided.

SINGLE AND DOUBLE BREEDERS.

Although we have mentioned single and double breeding cages, we are, for choice, decidedly in favour of devoting one of the double pattern to each pair of birds when space will permit. A single breeding cage consists of one compartment only, fitted with the necessary appliances for breeding with one pair of birds. But, as will be seen, there is no convenience for easily separating the cock from the hen, if that becomes necessary, nor for separating the young from their parents, save by employing a small cage (termed a "nursery" cage), which is hung on to the wires in front of the breeding cage.

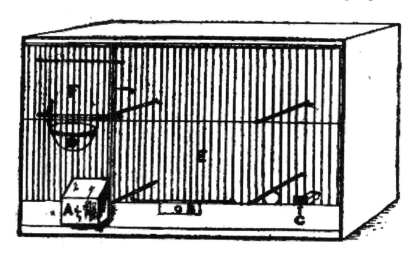

Modern Single Breeding Cage.

A—Seed Hopper. B—Egg Drawer. C—"Finger" Drawer for tit-bits.
D—Nest Pan. E—Slide-up Door. F—Door for removal and inspection of nest pan.

On the other hand, the double breeding cage, though virtually of the same pattern as a single one, is about double the size, and is divided into two compartments by a partition at the middle; each compartment being fitted with appliances for breeding. The partition dividing the compartments has a large (usually square) opening in it, by means of which the birds can be given the run of both compartments, or they may be kept separated (one in each compartment) by means of a wired slide which is made to run in grooves from the front and fit over the hole in the partition. When thus separated the birds can see and feed each other through the wires of the slide, or the parents can feed the young after separation. In most double breeders now, the central partition is made entirely removable, to enable the cage to be converted into one large compartment at will. This sliding division may be regarded as an advantage, especially where space is limited, as it enables one to give the birds a greater amount of exercise after breeding operations are over. It will thus be seen that a double breeding cage is practically two single ones built together and communicating with one another, so that the birds may at will be allowed to run together or be separated; or that they may be given the run of both compartments at once or limited to either the one or the other. In size a single breeding cage is usually about 20in. long, 16in. high, and 10in. deep; the double pattern is usually from 36in. to 40in. long, and about the same height and depth as a single one.

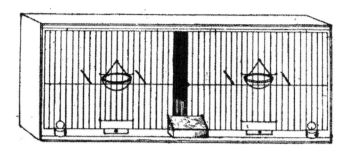

Modern Double Breeding Cage.

Fitted Ready to Commence Breeding.

A movable front should always be fitted to the cages. When the removable wire fronts are not used, the whole of the front with its wooden frame should be nailed on lightly (or, better still, screwed), so that it may be easily removed to allow free access to the inside for cleaning or whitewashing.

Sand drawers, or trays, should also be fitted to every cage. These are a sort of tray made of wood (or tin) with sides about half an inch deep, made to fit loosely in the bottom of each compartment, and having a piece of wood across the front to match the front of the cage. Knobs or wire handles are fixed on to allow of them being drawn in and out. The trays slide in at the bottom of the front piece of the cage, a space being left for the purpose. These sand drawers not only assist in the cleaning operations, but they allow the cleaning to be carried out with the least possible amount of disturbance to the birds, which is an important consideration during the breeding season.

POINTS TO AVOID.

In some, generally the cheaper, kinds of breeding cages the sand trays are omitted and a "turn-rail" is provided. This consists of a simple strip of wood to fit in the vacant space across the cage front (it may be said to represent the front of the sand tray). This strip is fixed in position by passing a wire through it near one end, and into the cage front, thereby forming a pivot, on which the rail turns outwards to allow the scraper to be passed into the cage to rake out husks and dirt. Metal scrapers and brushes with long thin handles are sold for this purpose. But it will be readily seen that the cages can scarcely be cleaned so thoroughly as when the tray may be entirely drawn out; besides, the operation causes a greater amount of disturbance to the birds, which might prove very detrimental during the breeding season.

Still another (and much more objectionable) style of cage has not even this convenience for carrying out cleaning efficiently, the wood front piece, to which the seed and water vessels are hung, being continued solid to the very bottom; so then the only means of scraping the bottom and removing dirt is by the door. Needless to say, the disturbance to the birds when cleaning operations are in progress reaches its highest point in this type of cage, as also does the danger from insanitary conditions. A man would be much more likely to breed disease germs and death in these cages than birds. One may succeed for a short time, but sooner or later (and it is generally sooner) disaster follows, and the cages which were so cheap in the beginning prove costly investments in the end.

CHAPTER II

PERCHES AND OTHER FITMENTS

So much for the breeding cage. Having decided upon the style and type, the next consideration will be the necessary appliances. It will suffice to describe the usual fitments of one compartment, which will serve as a model for the rest. Perches naturally claim first notice. These are usually three in number; two in the upper part of the cage, running from back to front and resting on the cross-bar of the cage-front, and one below, running from end to end and near the front, in such a position that the birds can easily reach their food and water. The size will vary according to the size of the birds kept. Half-inch, five-eights, and three-quarters are all good widths, according to the size of the birds, while three-eights to half-inch is a good depth. Don't make the mistake of having perches too wide and thick, especially for young birds, as nothing is more conducive to "slipped back claws." They should be of just such a thickness as will enable the birds to get a strong and firm grip of them, so that they may travel about them confidently. Remember, too, that an unstable and loose fitting perch is often the cause of unfertile eggs and failure in breeding. But although the perches must fit firmly and solid, they must never be made fast (as fixtures), for it is very advisable to remove and wash or scrape them clean at frequent intervals.

Following, in due order, the list of fittings for starting breeding:—The seed box—or hopper, as it is sometimes called—may be placed first in order, to point out that on a double breeding cage this appliance is placed in the centre of the cage, so that one half hangs each side of the central partition, and thus the one seed box serves both compartments. Then come the water vessels; one is hung on outside at opposite ends of the cage. Egg drawers also must be got, and these should slide in a hole in the middle of the cage front; one or two finger drawers to be used in the wires as required; a nest box or pan—with bracket, if required, for placing the pan in position; a nest bag to provide the birds with material for making the nest; and a piece of cuttle-fish bone.

In our accompanying illustration the front of a modern two-compartment breeding cage, and the arrangement of all the necessary feeding vessels is clearly shown. The seed-hopper fits on in front of the sliding partition which, as has been previously explained, divides the cage into two compartments or enables it to be turned into one big flight cage at will. As a rule, two holes are arranged in each compartment for the birds to put their heads through when feeding, but one only is placed over the water vessel. The seed box shown has the sloping top made of glass, but sometimes the back is made of that material, in each case for the purpose mentioned a little further on in my article. The egg-drawers will be seen fitting through a hole cut for the purpose in the cage front. The water vessels are of the latest "top hat" pattern, with every corner rounded off to facilitate thorough cleansing. In glass, these water vessels are to be obtained with covered tops, which help to keep out dust, seed husks, and the like. In the illustration one long sand tray (or drawer) is shown. Sometimes this tray is divided to make a separate one for each compartment. In a three-compartment breeding cage there is usually a tray for each part.

To prevent any misapprehension on the part of even the youngest beginner, we will take these appliances in order and add a few brief details.

SEED BOX.

Should be made of wood, with a sloping cover to throw off any dirt that may drop on it, and have a piece of glass for the back (that is, the front from an observer's point of view, when the box is hanging on the cage). The object of having this portion made of glass is two-fold; it enables the owner to see at a glance the amount of seed in the box, and the birds to see their food better when feeding. The part to hold the seed need not exceed an inch in depth.

WATER VESSELS.

Too well-known under the popular term "fountains" to need further description. Only glazed china, or glass vessels should be used, and these should be as free as possible from all corners and angles, so as to enable the insides to be cleaned perfectly. The glass vessels with covered tops and rounded bottoms and corners are, perhaps, about the best, as the upper portion almost entirely excludes all dirt and dust entering the water and fouling it.

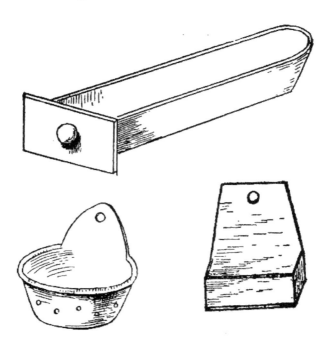

Finger Drawer.

Earthenware Nest Pan.   Wood Nest Box.

21

EGG DRAWER.

This is practically a small pot or china dish about $2\frac{1}{2}$ ins. to 3ins. long, $2\frac{1}{2}$ in. wide, and three-quarters of an inch deep. They are made in a variety of shapes (square, or with the back rounded, etc.), and are usually inserted in a hole provided for them just beneath the door of the cage, though in some cases where sliding wire doors are used the egg drawer is placed underneath the door, and there is a slot in the egg-drawer to allow the door to fall into it. Their use is to give the birds egg food, or any other soft or moist food that may be necessary. Here, again, only those with a smooth glazed china surface and quite free from any sharp angles or deep corners which cannot be kept perfectly clean should be at all tolerated.

The above three appliances, with a nest box or pan, and sometimes a nest bag, are the usual accompaniments of the breeding cages sold as being "fitted for breeding." I may mention, too, in passing, that these appliances may usually be found illustrated in the advertisement (Appliance) column of *Cage Birds*; while most dealers stock them.

FINGER DRAWER.

This may be described as a tiny edition of the egg drawer. It is made narrow enough to pass in between the wires, in which it fits rather tightly, when the pressure of the wires should be sufficient to hold the drawer in position. It is used to give any special food which one desires to give separately and in small quantities. These drawers are pushed in between the wires in any part of the cage that is most convenient—generally near the ends of the perches.

THE NEST BOX OR PAN.

The receptacle for holding the nest. It is made of quarter-inch wood, about $2\frac{1}{2}$ ins. deep, three inches square at bottom, and about $3\frac{1}{2}$ in. by $3\frac{1}{4}$ in. at the top. The front and two sides are placed on in a rather sloping position, whilst the back is nailed on at a right angle, and made a couple of inches higher. This surplus at the back being rounded off, and a hole bored in near the top, affords a very secure means of suspending the box in position without the use of a bracket. Our old friend the wood nest box is still a very useful servant, but is now very largely supplanted by the modern earthenware nest pan. The latter may well be described as a small shallow basin, made of earthenware, and pierced with holes for ventilating the nest and preventing sweating of the young. Some kinds (as the one illustrated) are made with an earthenware back, with a hole for suspending, which does away with the necessity for using wire brackets for the latter purpose. They are also sold with or without linings of either swansdown or felt. Most fanciers use these linings, and they are of great service with hens which build slovenly nests, or have to have nests made for them. Their use will be more fully described later.

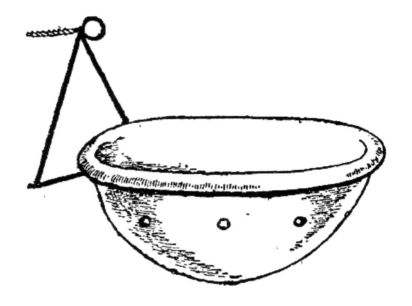

Modern Earthenware Nest Pan.

Showing Method of Hanging.

BRACKETS.

Usually provided with nest pans that are made without backs; and are also to be bought separately. They are simply brackets made of wire to hang in the cage and hold the nest pan. It should be seen that they are sufficiently stout, so that the weight of the pan does not render them shaky when a bird alights thereon.

NESTING MATERIALS.

The nest bag is not really a bag at all, but just a simple small bundle of suitable materials to make the nest. A type of nest bag sold at most corn and seed-dealers, who stock bird foods, is composed of a little soft hay, moss, and cow-hair. When it is required for use the bag may either be suspended to the wires of the cage, or placed in a wire rack, which can be purchased for the purpose, and hung in any convenient part of the cage. But there are some hens that waste a great deal more material than they use in the nest, by carrying it about the cage until they drop it on the floor, when they immediately turn to the "bag" and pull out a fresh supply.

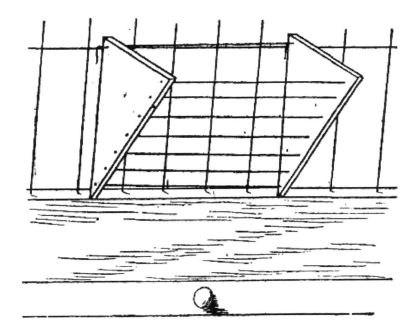

Rack for Holding Nesting Material.

Made of wood and wire, to hang on outside of cage.

A fancier, knowing his birds' peculiarities, would largely prevent this by withholding the nest bag until it was required for immediate use, and giving only a small supply of nesting material, stuck between the wires, until he saw that the hen was at work in real earnest to complete the nest. When this plan is carried out the coarser part of the nest bag is, of course, intended to be given first, and the finer material held back for the completion of the nest, in order to give it a snug and cosy finish. Other nesting materials may be bought separately by weight. Charpie is considered an excellent one, and is much used by German breeders, and cow-hair, both real and a manufactured substitute, may be bought separately. All these are sold at so much per pound weight. But with common birds, which are much more adept in the art of making a nest than the highly-bred fancy specimens, the common nest bags already described are very serviceable.

If the modern lined nest pans are used it naturally follows that little nesting material is required, but in every case it is advisable to give the hens a small quantity of the finer materials—cow-hair, charpie, or whatever else may be in use—as this gives the hens a chance to make some pretence at nest-building, and prevents them pulling the lining of the pan to pieces, which they are apt to do if every attempt at making a nest is denied to them. A piece of coarse string is sometimes tied on to a cage wire in a partly ravelled condition for the hens to pull to pieces, and thus distract their attention from the lining of the pan, and also to afford occupation to the wasteful type of hen mentioned above.

CUTTLEFISH BONE.

We now reach the last of our tabulated requirements—cuttlefish. Here again the term is rather a misnomer. What is termed cuttlefish is, in reality, only the limy solid portion of the bodies of those marine mollusca known as cuttlefish. It is, practically, wholly formed of lime, and, excepting the outer crust, is so soft that it can be easily scraped or even crushed between the fingers into powder. Its use is to provide the hens with limy matter for the formation of the shells of their eggs. It is, usually, in fair-sized flakes when sold, and a whole flake should be pierced with a hole and hung on the back of each cage, against the end of a perch.

Nearly all birds are fond of pecking at cuttlefish, and especially breeding hens, who will consume quite a large quantity. It should never be absent from a breeding-cage, and may be given with advantage at all seasons. It is also especially useful for young, growing birds. Cuttlefish may often be collected in large quantities on the sea coast, but it would be advisable to well wash any collected in this way before use. The properly dressed article, however, is so cheap that enough for a whole season may be bought for a few pence, so that one can scarcely be tempted on the score of cheapness to undertake the task of collecting and cleaning.

Having thus described a breeding cage in all its details, it is only necessary to add that it may be multiplied by as many units as is consistent with the breeder's inclinations, or the space at his disposal, provided that the appliances already described are increased in the same ratio as the cages themselves. Indeed, one should endeavour to always have in stock a few surplus appliances over the number required for actual use; then if it becomes necessary to remove or exchange any particular article for cleaning or any other purpose after the birds are put together, the exchange may be made without in any way dislocating one's general arrangements. For the same reason, it is also very advisable to adhere to one pattern throughout as far as possible, both for cages and appliances. One must always try to avoid the necessity of taking an appliance from one cage and immediately using it in or about another. Such a method is not without certain risks.

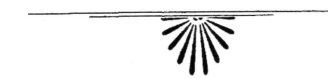

CHAPTER III

THE BIRD ROOM

We shall now have to decide where our operations will be carried on. If they are on a small scale, limited to, perhaps, two or three pairs of birds, and no spare room is available to accommodate our hobby, the cages will probably have to be hung in a kitchen, or ordinary dwelling-room, or, may be, the bedroom. Of the three we should prefer the latter, as the birds would be far less subject to disturbance by domestic operations, and this room is probably the, most equable in temperature and freest of draughts.

When one has no other choice but the kitchen or dwelling-room, the most important thing to avoid is hanging the cages high up near the ceiling. In this position the air is sure to be heated and impure, and when gas or lamp has been lit a few hours it becomes little short of poisonous. The cages should never be hung higher than the level of the gas jet when lit. This will not only ensure a purer atmosphere, but will afford the birds more light. A well-lighted position should always be preferred to a dull and dismal one. Another point to consider will be the burning of fires. If a fire is left burning through the night the usual great extremes of temperature will, in a measure, be avoided, but where this is not the case then it will be better to arrange the cages on the side of the room opposite to the fire-place if it can be done without encountering the draught of doors, as it will be seen at once that in these circumstances the nearer the birds are to the fire during the day the greater will be the drop in temperature they will have to endure at night when the fires are extinguished.

When one is starting on a larger scale, and has the advantage of a special room for the birds, the room should be properly arranged before making a start. If a choice of aspect is to be had (though few there are in such a happy position) it should be a bright and well-lighted, and still more important, a well-ventilated one. A room facing east or south-east, which gets the early morning sun, and is sheltered from the sun at mid-day, is an, ideal one. Look first to, the ventilation; see that there is ample ingress for fresh pure air, preferably low down near the floor, and an egress for impure air near the ceiling.

In lieu of any other means of ventilation it is a good plan to remove one or two panes of glass from the bottom row in the window, and as many from the top row, and nail over each vacancy two pieces of perforated zinc, placing one piece on the outside of the window frame and the other on the inside, and arranging them so that the perforations in the two sheets do not coincide with each other. If properly arranged, one will find that when looking directly forward at the one sheet of zinc, one only sees through the perforations the solid parts of the zinc sheet that is behind. This simple plan forms a very tolerable method of ventilation, and almost entirely does away with draught. Indeed, if a rather finely perforated zinc is used, draughts will be practically non-existent, and the interchange of air between the room and open air may go on continually at all times.

Next, the wall and ceiling should be limewashed, any paper that may be on being stripped off previously. If the cold glare of the whitewash is objected to, then a coloured distemper is preferable to paper, as the latter is too apt to form harbours for insect pests. The same consideration as to baffling these pests would suggest as an ideal dressing for the floor a simple beeswax and turpentine polish.

Along one or more sides of the room, staging should be erected for the accommodation of the cages. This should be placed in such a position as to receive the best of the light the room can afford, consistent, of course, with freedom from any possible draughts, and if that position should receive the early morning sun so much the better it will be. The staging may be of a simple kind, but it must be fixed up firmly and securely enough to withstand the highest strain that may be placed upon it, and its extent must be governed entirely by one's individual needs.

FURNISHING.

If one starts with a number of cages they may, with advantage, be grouped together tier above tier along one side of the room, provided one does not heap on tiers until the top rows are in the vitiated atmosphere that prevails near the ceiling. Four tiers should be the limit under all ordinary circumstances when starting from a staging about two feet high. In every case where one tier of cages is placed above another, the staging should be provided with shelves to carry each tier just clear of the one below, so that if it should become necessary to remove a cage from its place during the breeding season, it can be drawn out from its place without disturbing any of its neighbours, and returned again when required, or another of the same size and pattern may be substituted. This is one of the advantages of adhering to one particular pattern or style when starting the hobby, and of keeping a few surplus things on hand. It is advantageous in many ways, besides giving a more trim and uniform appearance to the room.

Few things are really necessary for furnishing the room, though it may be turned into a sanctum to which one may repair for a quiet hour, and in that case it will naturally become as elaborate as one's tastes or finances go. But even in this case one should aim at keeping the room as plainly and simply furnished as possible. A corn or seed bin in which the seeds and foods are stored is the first consideration. In this the seed should be kept separately, and mixed as required for use, and the bin should be made secure from mice. A good plan is to keep the seed in tins with closely-fitting lids, the tins being labelled with the name of the contents, and stored together in the bin. A cupboard in the bird room is quite a luxury for neatly storing away small surplus appliances, as well as baths, bottles, disinfectants, and the many little things used daily, which would otherwise give an untidy aspect to the general appearance of the room.

Egg Grater.

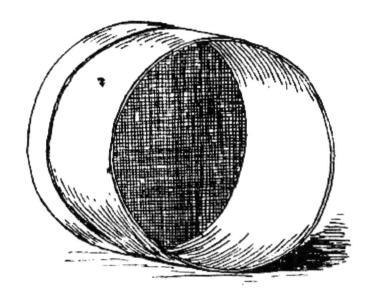

Seed Sieve.

A chair or two and table are great conveniences in the bird room—the latter may well be regarded as an essential feature, as, without it, it is difficult at times to carry on properly all the operations of mixing and preparing food. Of the many little articles we may mention in the course of the season, let it suffice here to give a brief catalogue of the principal things which should be ready at hand from the start. A basin and jug, or two of each, spoon, fork, bread-grater, egg-sieve, seed-crusher, seed-cleaner—which may be combined with the egg-sieve—baths; and a small bellows distributor for spraying insect powder into crevices or sharp angles will be useful. Egg-racks, sprays, and a few other articles, may be regarded as coming more in the scope of luxuries, though they are decidedly useful, if not quite essential. A nice, healthy growing shrub or two in pots may also be classed in the latter category, but the extra tone they add to the snug and cheerful appearance of the room more than repays the small amount of trouble they require to keep them flourishing.

THE QUESTION OF TEMPERATURE.

In a room entirely devoted to one's hobby a small thermometer should always find a place if it is intended to make use of any form of artificial heat. A serviceable instrument may be bought for little more than a shilling, or a good reliable one, for about half-a-crown. But, on the whole, the beginner would be well advised to eschew all artificial aids of that kind, and aim at producing only such birds as are well able to live happily and enjoy life in a normal temperature. He may find it difficult when first starting with well-bred stock to carry such a resolution into effect, but the difficulties will vanish as soon as he takes the precaution to assure himself beyond doubt that the birds he starts with have been bred and reared under natural conditions as regards temperature.

Still, this is but one view of a disputed question, and although convinced that it is based on sound principles, I must, in order to help those who would be of another school, refer briefly to the other side of the question. The ideal source of heat would undoubtedly be a fire in an ordinary open grate, as by this method heat and ventilation must in great measure go together to ensure the proper burning of the fire. Very few, however, are able to avail themselves of this method, which requires very constant attention. It would also be necessary to enclose the fireplace with a wire screen to prevent a tragedy should a bird escape from its cage. A system of hot-water pipes, with the source of heat placed outside in the open air, is the next in order, and is certainly the most efficient and generally applicable method. But in this method it must be remembered that ventilation is not promoted in the least (on the contrary, the atmosphere is more apt to become stagnant); therefore, it is more than usually imperative that the system of ventilation be made very efficient. Of the least desirable means of heating may be placed in due order slow combustion stoves, portable hot-water coils, which usually require heating over a gas jet, and gas or oil stoves, fitted with atmospheric burners.

VENTILATION THE PRIMAL NECESSITY.

Whatever the method adopted, the first and prime consideration is to see that the ventilation is of the best, and in the case of gas or oil stoves, that these are provided with a cover and flue to carry the fumes and products of combustion out of the room—either into the open air or into some adjacent chimney flue. In either case the end of this flue must have a cover or cap over it to prevent the possibility of a down-draught.

Whatever kind of stove is used within the room, the centre of the room will almost invariably be the best position for it from an economic point of view, and to ensure heating all parts of the room alike. Another word before parting with this subject for a time. It is this: Put not your trust in stoves that are reputed to neither smoke nor smell, for such an idealistic appliance has, in my opinion, yet to be invented. Look upon them always as risky and dangerous servants, for only in this way lies safety. When properly installed, let the thermometer be a guide to the necessity of increasing the normal temperature. As long as it keeps above 45 degrees there is no need whatever to increase it.

CHAPTER IV

ABOUT THE BATH

Before returning to the birds, a few remarks may be devoted to the bath. As probably everyone knows, the Canary is, given the opportunity of being so, a cleanly creature, and preserves its cleanliness of plumage almost solely by bathing in water, so that the bath is an indispensable appliance. One type, which may be obtained for a few pence, is made on the same principle as the seed-box, but with wires in the top to hang on the front of the cage in the open doorway. This type can be very easily made by anyone, and, if covered with two or three coats of bath enamel, which will prevent the water soaking into the wood to cause leakage, will be as good as those one can buy. In this way some excellent baths may be made out of the wood of cigar boxes.

Bath Cage—Hung in Position.

The only objection to this style of bath is that at times vigorous bathers will splash the water into the cage. But this is easily remedied by withdrawing the sand drawers whilst giving the bath. This ensures the inside of the cage being dry for the birds. Other types of baths are simply shallow pans, an inch or so in depth, and round, square, or oval in shape. It is necessary to place this bath in a small cage, similar to a nursery cage without the perches, and without wires in one end, which is then hung on the open doorway, as above. This is doubtless the best means of keeping the living cage nice and dry, but, as will be seen, it increases both the stock of appliances, and, to some extent, the labour.

HOW TO DISTINGUISH SEX

We will now suppose one has everything in readiness for the stock of birds. In settling about the buying of the stock, the first question that will puzzle the beginner will, in all probability, be the sexing of his purchases. In dealing with any respectable dealer one will be far safer in trusting to the vendor's judgment than endeavouring to settle such a matter oneself, so that it is only for the benefit of those who buy and select their birds locally that we will endeavour to help them to sex their purchases. Even when buying in the former way, the novice will be well advised to ask the help of some experienced fancier friend, and not to expect infallibility in every instance from the most time-worn expert. As a matter of fact, all outward sexual differences in the Canary are practically obliterated, so that it is more a kind of instinct born of experience and observation which enables a fancier to tell the sex of a bird at a glance.

In comparison, a cock will be found to have a bolder and more jaunty manner than a hen, the eye fuller and bolder; and in clear or lightly-marked birds the throat just at the base of the under beak will generally be of a brighter tone of yellow. The "tweet" of the cock has also a bolder and more defiant ring, and when he sings the throat swells out and pulsates or palpitates very plainly. Some hens will "sing" very tolerably, but in their case the song is disconnected, and there is rarely much trace of the pulsation of the throat which is such a feature of the song of the cock. In the hen the "song" is really more in the nature of a more or less sustained twitter. To the young beginner all differences are very subtle, and he need not feel discouraged if he fails for a time to recognise them in a given bird. A keener insight will grow up after learning to distinguish them by comparing two or more birds together at one time.

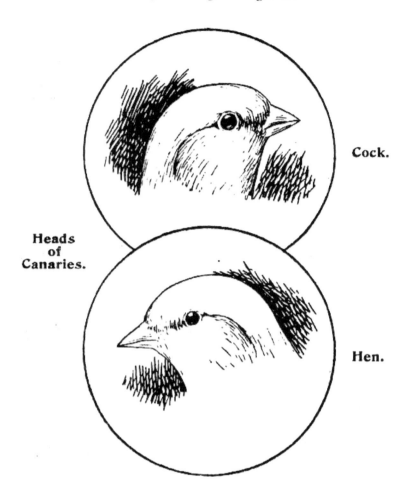

Cock.

Heads
of
Canaries.

Hen.

When the birds are in breeding condition there is another difference which the veriest novice might easily recognise. This is in the external appearance of the vent. If the birds are caught and the feathers of the abdomen blown aside, the vent of the cock will be quite prominent and rather pointed, whilst that of the hen is flatter, almost level with the abdomen, and more expansive in appearance. This is perhaps the best guide for the novice who has to rely on his own judgment, but it must be borne in mind that it is only whilst the birds are in breeding condition that this difference is of a very marked character. After the breeding season is over—and in birds that do not come into breeding condition—the difference is not very marked. Neither is it a reliable guide to tell the sex of young birds until the following spring, when they will be coming into condition.

TAKE CARE, AND TIME.

Having got over these initial difficulties and procured the requisite stock of birds, one will naturally be anxious to set them up in house-keeping. Here, however, one cannot too thoroughly absorb and digest the wisdom of these two small maxims—"Proceed carefully," and "more haste, less speed." Putting the birds together before they are in the proper condition, and stimulating them into condition too early, are doubtless the causes of more losses and disappointment than all other causes put together.

When kept under normal conditions and not stimulated by the too free use of egg-food or rich oily seeds, the birds will not, as a rule, show signs of desiring to go to nest until about the middle of March, which is quite early enough to begin. But when the operations are carried on in a heated kitchen it is not always possible to restrain the birds so long. The most that can be done in these circumstances is to limit the diet to a staple of canary seed, with a pinch of niga twice a week for the hens, a teaspoonful of rape twice a week for the cocks, and a little bread and milk once a week all round. Green food or a piece of apple should be given daily.

Then when the birds come into breeding condition it is better to take the risk and mate them. If the day and night temperature are fairly equable all will probably go on well, let the season be what it may. Indeed, it is almost invariably in a warm kitchen where fires are left burning at night that one hears of unusually early young being reared. But the breeder who keeps his birds under different conditions and in unheated rooms must not be deluded into trying to emulate the example of early mating and put his birds together too early, or he is practically certain to meet with a grievous disappointment.

FOOD WHEN PREPARING FOR BREEDING.

Birds being prepared for breeding may be given a more liberal diet by adding a fourth proportion of German rape to the staple food. Next, make a mixture of equal parts of hemp, maw, niga, and linseed, and give a small teaspoonful of this mixture to the cocks every second day, and to the hens twice a week. A teaspoonful of egg food or crushed biscuits should also be given to the cocks twice a week, and the hens once a week. This question of egg food is notoriously a thorny one, so I propose to dismiss it briefly here, in order to deal with it more fully a little further on. A spray of green food should be given daily, when the weather is favourable for gathering. Do not, however, give greenstuff that is gathered in wet or frosty weather, unless it has first lain indoors for an hour or two; better still, do not give it at all.

While the birds are being thus brought into condition the breeder should take the precaution to overhaul the breeding cages in a final inspection. See that all the fittings—seed and water vessels, egg drawers, sand trays, etc.—are securely in their places, and yet slide in and out without jambing, that the perches are firm and secure, and a piece of cuttlefish and nest pan firmly fixed in place. The position I like best for the nest pan is on the back of the cage, midway between, and on a level with, the two upper perches, because the hens generally prefer the little extra seclusion which this position affords, and also because the pan will hang more free of the perches. When it is hung on the side of the cage the perch is usually quite close up to the front of the pan, and is apt to tempt lusty young birds out of the nest too soon. The only objection to the pan being at the back is that one cannot peep into it so easily, which is, perhaps, a point in its favour after all, as the novice should cultivate from the beginning the habit of interfering with the birds as little as possible.

CHAPTER V

FIRST PRINCIPLES IN MATING

Whilst the birds are being prepared for mating it is well to also utilise the interval by going carefully over their good and bad points, and come to a decision as to which birds shall form each pair. It is not in the province of these articles to enter into the pros and cons of pedigree breeding, or the cultivation of fancy points. There are, however, just a few general principles which it is better to keep in view from the very first start in the art of breeding Canaries.

The chief of these may be roughly divided into two classes (1) That two birds both possessing glaring faults (and especially two possessing the same glaring fault), or any point it is not wished to reproduce in the young, should never be mated together; (2) that birds of the same colour should not be bred together. Of course these, and particularly the latter, are but broad, general principles from which the experienced breeder deems it advisable at times to deviate, but all such considerations come more within the scope of the fancier who has passed the stage when learning to breed and rear a bird of some kind.

The breeder, however, who wishes to raise good sized birds (good in substance and stout in body) must not expect to do so by mating together two puny, undersized specimens. He must have plenty of size to begin with in one, if not in both, of the birds forming each pair. Similarly, if he desires to breed clear birds, he cannot expect them to turn up, except an occasional sport, as it were, from the mating of heavily marked or green birds.

As regards the "two colours" mentioned, they are termed respectively yellow and buff, and they exist in every variety of marking and variegation, from the first breaking up of the self-green colour. It will suffice to describe the difference between the two types as it is to be observed in clear or lightly marked birds. In yellows, although the depth of colour may vary in tone from pale lemon to a rich orange, the colour is continued right to the edge of the web of the feather, whereas, in the buff type the yellow colour stops just short of the edge, leaving a narrow margin of white around the edge of the feathers, which gives a frosted appearance to the bird's plumage, as though its yellow colour was dusted over with white powder. The distinction is splendidly shown in the coloured plate of Cinnamon Canaries issued with *Cage Bird's* 1906 Special Spring Number. This buff plumage is also called "mealy."

In selecting the breeding stock one should mate a yellow

with a buff, and refrain from "double-yellowing," or "double-buffing"—which means mating together two yellows or buffs, as the case may be—until some experience has been gained. In a general way the yellows give colour and quality of feather; the buffs size and substance of body and profusion of feather. It will also materially help to keep up the natural depth of colour in the young if one of the parents is a variegated bird. It should be known that the real source of all natural colour is the Green, but beyond mentioning the simple fact we need not touch further upon the subject here.

PAIRING UP THE BIRDS.

All these preliminaries of inspection and selection being completed, the hens should be placed in their breeding quarters, the latter fully equipped for breeding, with the sole exception of the nest bag, which must be withheld until the birds are properly mated and ready to at once begin nesting. The cocks should be placed in separate cages and hung beside their respective partners, in full view of each other, and in such a position that the cock can feed the hen between the wires when so disposed.

One of the advantages of using a double-breeding cage for each pair of birds is that the hen may be placed in one compartment and the cock in the other, with only the wired partition separating them. When the birds have been kept in this way for a few days, and the cock is seen frequently calling the hen to the wired slide and giving her food, it is only necessary to take out the slide and to allow them to begin nesting.

Mating the Birds.

On the other hand, when single cages are used, it is always advisable (and often quite necessary) to place the cock in a small cage, such as a nursery cage, and hang it on the front of the cage containing the hen for a day or two before finally putting them together. Serious quarrelling often results by introducing them to each other too suddenly.

Except under such special circumstances as previously pointed out (where the birds are kept in a warm situation) the latter end of March is quite early enough to carry out the work just described, and the last few days in March or first week of April will be early enough to finally put the birds together. This leaves an interval of about ten days during which time the birds should still be given the more generous diet already advised. A small leaf of dandelion daily will be of great value, and a pinch of inga seed every second day given in the finger drawer, to the hen only, will be invaluable as a preventative of egg-binding.

If all goes well, not many days should elapse, after getting the birds to this stage, before they are ready for mating, and whether the period be long or short, it is not only advisable to run them together as soon as they reach the proper condition, but it is also essential that they should be kept apart until that condition of fitness is arrived at. No good can come of putting together birds that have no desire for mating.

SIGNS OF BREEDING CONDITION.

But how is the beginner to know when the birds are in the proper condition? Given birds in normal health the signs are not easily mistakeable. And here let me digress for a moment to say to the novice that one of the most vital principles that lead to success in breeding in the early days of one's connection with the hobby is to rigidly weed out and reject weakly, unhealthy stock birds. To return to the subject of mating. When the cock is seen frequently popping down to the wires next the hen's compartment and calling vigorously to her, and giving her food out of his beak when she goes to him, filling up the remainder of his time singing violently to her, he is in the proper condition for mating; as also is the hen when she is seen travelling about the perches restlessly and excitedly, and responding quickly and freely to the "calls" of the cock, and occasionally pulling at a beakful of her breast feathers, which she may make some pretence at carrying about and placing in the nest pan or upon the end of a perch. At this stage she is apt to steal a few feathers from the cock bird whenever she gets an opportunity to grab a beakful of his plumage.

It is now that just a beakful of nesting material, or even a single feather, or a bit of partly ravelled string tied on the wires is sometimes useful to prevent her plucking her mate or herself. But when both birds exhibit the symptoms just detailed no time should be lost in putting them together— they will doubtless begin nesting at once.

In some cases it is quite as harmful to keep the birds apart when they have arrived at a "ripe condition" as it is to mate them before they are ready. Whereas, if they are put together at the proper time (excepting, perhaps, in odd cases, which only go to prove the rule) all else will follow as a matter of course, and the birds will frequently be commencing to sit upon their first nest of eggs at the end of a fortnight from the time the slides were finally withdrawn.

CHAPTER VI

BUILDING THE HOME

When the slides are withdrawn, and the birds first gain access to each other, the action of the cock birds will vary greatly. Whereas one will perhaps take little notice of the hen for a time, another will quietly sidle up to her and commence feeding her in a few minutes, and still another will burst immediately into violent song before the hen, and finish up by chasing her about the cage in such a way as to make the beginner think a fierce battle is being fought. But such is not the case, and, on the whole, this vehement style of courtship (for it is really nothing else) is a favourable omen, as it shows the birds are in full vigour and high condition. The birds will usually quickly settle down, and "work off steam" at nest building. Of course, all this does not imply that those birds which act in the reverse manner are not in condition for breeding; but in all ordinary cases the vigorous wooers will generally be found to settle down to business more quickly than their lackadaisical neighbours.

The day after putting the birds together, the cock may be

observed frequently getting into the nest pan and "calling" to the hen, using all his wiles to tempt her into it. If the hen is also seen plucking at her breast, or carrying about a feather or bit of material that has been given her to play with, taking it in and out of the nest-pan, it will be time to give her a little nesting material, beginning with the coarser parts of the nest bag. If she appears to be at work in earnest, taking the material into the nest pan and leaving it there, more may be given as required until a nice comfortable nest is made.

It is at this stage that one will see the reason for withholding the nesting material until the birds are really beginning to feel the necessity for a nest, because most hens will go on building until about to lay the first egg, and some will work energetically until the second, third, or even fourth egg is deposited, and if the material is given too soon, so that the nest is completed some days before the hen will lay, the supply of material will almost invariably have to be kept up, thus enabling the hen to build up a needlessly bulky nest; or, failing that, she will drag out the nest she has already made and begin over again with the same material. This not only causes much unsightly litter and waste of material, but, in my opinion, often has the effect of making a hen a slovenly builder. Therefore, whether the period be a day or a week after the birds are first put together before they show signs of being in real want of a nest, as already described, the material should be withheld, save for just a tuft of cowhair or a feather or two to amuse the hen.

HELP WHEN NEST BUILDING.

Although common-bred hens are as a rule much more expert architects than their more highly-bred sisters, one must not expect to find every lady capable of getting along without assistance. At the same time, whatever assistance is rendered should be well-timed and not premature. The cosily-lined pans that are made in these days largely dispense with the necessity of having a certain amount of material in the pan before an egg is laid, for, if the lining is properly secured around the sides of the pan before being placed in the cage, there will be practically no danger of an egg being broken even if laid in the pan before any material has been deposited. The best method is to supply the material as already advised and then leave the, hen to her own resources until she has laid her third egg; or, in the event of unlined pans or nest boxes being used, until the evening of the day before she is expected to lay her first egg. Then, if she has shown herself unable to construct a passable nest, take the matter in hand and do the work for her.

Nothing is easier than to make a nest if you go about it

in the right way. It is best to do this in the evening after the birds have settled down to roost; further, it is better to have a spare pan or box, of the same pattern as the one in the cage, in which to construct the nest, and thus reduce disturbance of the birds to a minimum. A wood block for making a nest can be bought at most dealers for a copper or two, but a small earthenware or china ball is just as good, whilst neither can surpass a hard-boiled hot egg—perhaps just been boiled in readiness for the birds' breakfast next morning.

MAKING A NEST.

To make the nest, get the nest pan or box, as the case may be, a supply of nesting material, and a hard-boiled egg which has cooled only just enough to enable you to handle it. If the pan is a lined one only a little cowhair will be required. Take the requisite quantity, pluck it out lightly with the fingers to remove any hard, knotty, portions, and drop it into the pan so that it fills the pan evenly all over. Now take the hot egg and place the thick end in the centre of the cowhair and press it lightly down, twisting the egg round in the meanwhile, until it is sunk in the mass of hair as deep as the finished nest should be. Leave the egg in position while you arrange the ridge of the cowhair neatly around the edge of the pan; then give a few more turns to the egg and lift it out. The result will be a beautifully-shaped nest of a very nice size for the average Canary, and it will retain its shape far better than any nest shaped with the fingers or any cold instrument. The, reason is that the heat of the egg moulds the hair into the shape required.

When the unlined pans or the common wooden boxes are used, the above procedure need only be varied by placing some of the coarser material of which the nest bag is composed into the receptacle before adding the cowhair. This portion of material may be roughly shaped out with the fingers, the hair being then placed in position and moulded as already described. The square wooden nest boxes require a much larger amount of material in the making of a nest than the ordinary nest pan; but a proportionately larger amount of the coarse material may be used in filling up the corner spaces, leaving plenty of room for a good substantial lining of cowhair.

Of course, in every case where cowhair is mentioned it may be taken to apply equally to charpie, or any other substitute for cowhair that may be in use. The nest being made and ready, quietly exchange it for the one in the cage just after the birds have settled down to roost, when they will more readily accept the new order of things and refrain from pulling the nest to pieces, as so often happens when it is given in the early part of the day, or before the hen is ready to lay.

During the interval between putting the birds together and egg-laying, little, if any, change need be made in the diet. The usual seed diet supplemented by a very little egg-food once or twice a week, and a spray of green food daily is quite sufficient, But do not omit giving a pinch, of inga seed in a finger drawer once or twice a week until the hen has laid. As a preventive of egg-binding it is excellent. As regards the best kinds of green food, the opinions of practical breeders are so varied that one would be well advised to adhere to that kind which gives good results in one's own hands. Personally, I would give preference to chickweed, groundsel, or watercress in the order named, reserving dandelion for such birds as were backward, or slow in coming into breeding condition. For the latter class of birds a leaf of dandelion daily is very useful, but the supply should cease when it is seen that the hens are getting near to egg-laying, and it should be discarded altogether for the rest of the season.

CHAPTER VII

THE FIRST EGG

Even the tyro will soon learn to discover when a hen is about to lay. As nest-building progresses the hen will be noticed calling from the nest more frequently to her mate, and a few days before she lays a keen observer will notice a slight fullness of the abdomen daily becoming more apparent. On the afternoon of the day before she lays her first egg a little less energy is usually shown both in nest-making and in courting the attention of the male bird.

Sometimes as the evening drags on a hen will begin to look quite dull and mopy. This is not altogether a favourable symptom, as it is often a premonition of egg-binding, so that in every such case one should make a point of looking at these hens early next morning—certainly before breakfast—in order to see if they are doing well. But do not interfere with them next morning even if they do not lay. Wait a few hours, or longer if the hens seem pretty lively, before attempting to treat them for egg-binding. In this connection it may be pardonable to refer one to the illustrated article on "Egg-Binding," which appeared in the columns of *Cage Birds* on March 3rd (No. 216), or to the pages of *Cage Bird's Annual*, before making any attempt to treat a hen for this complaint.

Even when a hen goes into the nest at roost time and stays there all night and until she has laid next morning, it does not follow as a matter of course that she is going to be egg-bound. Some hens have little idiosyncracies of this kind. Still, as long as the possibilities are there, it is well to be on guard, and assure oneself that things are going on satisfactorily.

REMOVING EARLY EGGS.

Supposing all goes well, and one finds an egg when looking into the nest on the all-important morning when it is expected. It is not much to look upon—just a little greyish-white object, closely freckled and sometimes a little spotted, especially about the larger end, with grey. Altogether an egg bearing a very close resemblance to that of the wild Linnet. Of course, this is the common type, for, as might be expected in such a purely domestic race of birds as our Canaries have become, there are variations in the shade of colour and marking. One will be lighter in ground colour than another; others coarser in freckling, and with more distinct spotting. The most curious lot I ever saw was a clutch of three I had laid by a Norwich hen, which had a very distinct band of "Hedge Sparrow blue" near the larger end, the rest of the ground colour being the usual greyish-white, and over all the usual grey freckling. This, however, was quite in the nature of a freak. One other curious fact may be noted; that the colour of the clutches of eggs will almost, if not quite invariably become of a lighter shade towards the end of the season.

Many breeders remove the eggs each morning as laid, and return them altogether on the evening of the third day. The object of this is to prevent the first young one being hatched two or three days before the last, as generally happens when the eggs are not removed, in consequence of the, hens beginning to incubate from the time the first egg is laid, so that in a clutch of four eggs (which is the most usual number) the one laid first has been incubating three days before the last one is laid. A clutch of eggs may number anything from two to eight. Both these are unusual numbers, but are frequently met with. The most frequent numbers are four and five, and four may safely be taken as an average, so that when the first three eggs are removed as they are laid and returned on the evening of the third day all will start fairly equal, and the young will generally all hatch out the same day and so have an equal start in life, which is not always the case when the hatching-out is spread over several days. Then the oldest birds gain much in size and strength before the last of the clutch are hatched, and shoulder their weaker nest-mates out of the way at feeding time until their own appetites are satiated, and if the hen happens to be a careless or indifferent feeder the youngest bird rarely gets well fed. But all this counts for very little when one has good feeding hens—and the commoner birds are amongst the very best as feeders—as the hen will go on feeding as long as the young birds continue to gape, and each birds gets properly fed from the start. In the latter case the younger ones rapidly gain on the elder ones, and by the time they leave, the nest will be indistinguishable as regards size.

If it is decided to remove the eggs a "nest egg" should be substituted for the first removed. One for each nest will suffice. These eggs may be purchased made in wood, which are, perhaps, better than china ones. Most Canaries, however, will be quite satisfied with anything bearing a faint resemblance to the size and shape of an egg. An unfertile egg from another nest is often used as a nest egg, in which case some little mark of identification should be placed upon it to prevent the possibility of mistaking it.

Needless to say, so fragile an object as a bird's egg requires very delicate handling. Fanciers' providers endeavour to solve the difficulty by supplying tongs or spoons specially made for picking up and removing eggs. But the average man will generally find his own fingers quite as safe an instrument as anything else, although he will need to use them gingerly to avoid a catastrophe.

Another point which must not be overlooked when the eggs are removed and several pairs of birds are kept, which may be breeding at the same time, is to number the cages consecutively, and then to get a shallow box, or tray, about an inch in depth and divided into as many sections as there are pairs of birds. Each section must be numbered to correspond with the numbers on the cages, and as the egg is removed each day from the cage it should be placed in the section of the tray bearing the number corresponding to that of the cage. This prevents any mistake of mixing up the eggs from different pairs. Each section of the tray should be half-filled with bran or cotton wool to prevent injury to the eggs.

CHAPTER VIII

COMMENCEMENT OF INCUBATION

In the evening of the day on which the third egg is laid look at the nest, and if badly made prepare a new nest (as already described in detail in the last chapter) dust it well underneath the material and around the sides (and in the corners if square boxes are used) with freshly ground pyrethrum powder. Then remove the nest-egg, put in the three eggs, and quietly place the nest in the cage. Should the nest be well constructed by the hen Canary and require no other attention, still give it a dusting with pyrethrum powder before returning the eggs. Next morning the fourth egg will probably be laid and incubation commence in real earnest. If a fifth or sixth egg should be deposited, such additions will have to take their chance, as they cannot be accurately forecasted, and after the first three have been duly replaced no further interference with either nest or bird should be attempted at this period.

Normally the eggs are laid in daily succession—one each day after the first is laid until the clutch is completed. There are exceptions to this rule in both directions; that is, cases where a hen occasionally misses laying one day (after laying one or two eggs) before completing the clutch; and cases are known where a hen has laid two eggs in one day. But for practical utility the hens that go by the general rule are the most satisfactory.

Incubation last fourteen days. In the second round of nests, when the weather is often very warm, and, perhaps, the vital forces most energetic, the period is often shortened several hours, so that the young may hatch on the thirteenth day.

When incubation has commenced a plain diet should be given. As a staple, canary seed with about a fourth part of summer rape will be quite sufficient, to which may be added a small quantity of egg-food once a week. Green food may be withheld during incubation without any ill result, and if given it should be only in very small quantities. This is not so much from fear of actual ill resulting from its use; but some hens will leave the nest very frequently and stay off too long at a time as long as fresh green food is in the cage, so that by giving it in unlimited quantities it may be the indirect cause of harm.

If the weather is bright and warm the bath may be hung on the cage for half an hour each morning to give the hen an opportunity of bathing when she leaves the nest for food and water; but in cold, chilly weather it is better to omit the bath whilst the hen is sitting. On the other hand if the weather is warm and dry toward the close of the incubatory period, it is a good plan to leave the bath on the cage for a couple of hours or so in the early part of the day; also to put it on for a similar period in the afternoon for the last two days before eggs are expected to hatch. If the hen bathes freely the moisture which she must carry into the nest on her feathers will aid the hatching process.

WHAT SHALL WE DO WITH HIM?

Another point which must be left largely to the discretion of the individual fancier is the question of removing the cock from the hen during the period of incubation. As with removing the eggs, opinions on this point differ diametrically, but in this case the temperament of the birds is a factor to reckon with. There are hens which will not so much as sit out the incubatory period if the cock is taken away, and others which will hatch the eggs, but make very indifferent mothers; yet either will both sit and rear the young with every satisfaction when the cock is left with them. Still others, and, perhaps, the largest proportion take little notice whether the cock is present or absent, and carry out their duties as well in either case.

Then it is sometimes necessary to remove the cock on

account of his propensity for being too meddlesome with the nest, which sometimes results in the nest being pulled to pieces or the eggs broken. Again there are cocks which will often go on the nest and cover the eggs quite matron-like when the hen comes off to feed or "stretch her legs," or which will go on and sit beside the hen. This kind of bird must not be mistaken for a mischievous, meddlesome cock, as he is often a very great help to a hen in rearing the young.

Of course, the moral of all this is that only the owner who knows his birds' idiosyncracies can tell with any degree of certainty whether it is best to leave the birds together whilst hatching and rearing are in progress. One thing, however, is certain: if the cock is removed, he should be placed out of sight of the hen. If double breeding cages are used and the cock is merely shut off by the wired slide, the probability is that he will create just as much trouble by disturbing the hen with his calls and enticing ways, which often succeed in tempting the hen to leave the nest much oftener that she would otherwise do, and spend much of her time at the wire partition "talking scandal" with her mate.

This may be prevented by using a solid wood slide as a partition in place of the wired one, or by pasting a piece of stout brown paper over the wired slide, which can be easily removed when it is not required. But on the whole the new beginner in the hobby may succeed best by allowing the birds to remain together and leave experiments severely alone. This, of course, is only intended to apply to the general rule. Mischievous cocks such as are described above, and a few other special cases which will be mentioned in due course, should certainly be separated and treated as described.

CHAPTER IX

EGG FOOD: A THORNY SUBJECT.

At this point, whilst the hen is engaged in the task of incubation, we will deal with the subject of egg-food. It is notoriously a thorny subject of late years, but I shall endeavour to give each method a fair consideration without prejudice or feeling whatever. Perhaps I had better have said "soft-food," since one small section, whose opinions are entitled to unprejudiced hearing, would discard egg in all forms from the birds' diet. I will consider the latter aspect first and say at once that their objections to egg are based on facts which have been proved by scientific experimentation.

Briefly, the objections are that egg is one of the very best—if not actually the best—of all cultivating media for the bacilli which cause that terrible scourge of the bird-breeder, septic fever. So it is during the breeding season, when the resistive powers of the birds to disease are lowered, that the septic bacilli, in so favourable a breeding ground as a constant supply of hard-boiled egg, are quickly bred up to an unusually dangerous degree of virility.

To remedy this we are told that egg should be cut out of the dietary. The simplicity of the remedy cannot be gainsaid. But there remains the question: Can we rear the same proportion of young from a given number of birds, quite irrespective of size and quality of young, without egg as with it? My own experience gave me a negative reply,

TO REAR WITHOUT EGG.

although I had experimented and fully proved the possibility of rearing Canaries without egg in any form long before the no-egg theory was publicly mooted. Thus, of its practicability in rearing high-class birds I have yet to be convinced.

However, I shall leave the breeder to settle the matter for himself, and if he wishes to go in for the no-egg method he may supply either of the following foods instead. First, in addition to the usual seeds, give a daily supply of crushed biscuit slightly moistened, and in a separate vessel a liberal allowance of cracked hemp, with which may be mixed a little dried fruit. Dried insects are practically useless unless the birds have been previously educated to eat them, as few Canaries will touch them so long as other food is available; when eaten they may prove useful. When young birds are four or five days old one may begin to add a little soaked rape seed to the biscuit food, and also give a daily supply of green food. One must bear in mind that soaked rape rapidly turns sour, even in a moderate temperature; therefore it must be prepared fresh every day—twice each day would be better—and only sufficient be given to last the day If any is left at night it should be thrown away and the egg drawers washed before putting in the supply for early morning feeding.

Another method of rearing without egg is to use an article known as prepared seeds as a substitute for egg-food. This substance, as its name implies, appears to be composed entirely of seeds and vegetable compounds, and only requires moistening with water. All the shells or husks of the seeds have been eliminated.

Still another method, which is, perhaps, the most satisfactory of all the no-egg systems is to employ crushed puppy biscuits as a substitute for egg and biscuit. Either cod-liver oil or cod-liver oil and malt brands which do not contain meat are the proper brands to use. When crushed finely and slightly moistened with water they form a really excellent and wholesome soft food, and there is no reason whatever why they should not rear strong, robust birds just as well as the orthodox egg-food. Indeed they have been used successfully for many years past by numbers of amateur breeders.

The fact remains, however, that practically all the principal breeders and exhibitors cling to the old method of egg and bread crumbs, or depart from this system only so far as to substitute biscuit powder for the bread crumbs. But the general concensus of opinion would probably be in favour of crumb of household bread. The heads of the Fancy, so to speak, do not seem to be troubled with visitation of septic fever to any greater extent than their humbler brethren. Of course, the explanation doubtless lies in the fact that these "leading lights" have immense advantages over the average amateur in the way of hygiene and healthful surroundings for their birds.

A MIDDLE COURSE.

But to steer a middle course between the egg and no-egg systems is a rather easier matter, and in most hands the method will succeed very well so far as concerns quantity and quality of results. This method consists in substituting the preserved yolk of egg which is sold under such divers names as preserved egg, desiccated egg, preserved yolk, egg flake, and several others, for the orthodox hard-boiled yolk of fresh eggs, and adding thereto the usual quantities of biscuit powder or bread crumbs.

A very good food which can be mixed in sufficient quantity to last a week may be made by crushing a pound of maizena wafer biscuits and adding half a pound of preserved egg flake.

Thoroughly mix all together and pack dry in a clean tin, or earthen jar with a close-fitting lid or cover. In this condition it will keep in perfectly good condition for a week or two. When required for use simply take out the required quantity and slightly moisten it with a few drops of water. Or crumb of stale household bread that has been soaked in water and squeezed nearly dry may be blended with it with a fork, and will moisten the whole sufficiently.

Of course, this food may be prepared in greater or less quantities by adhering to the same proportions of two parts crushed biscuit to one part of egg; but it is best to prepare only sufficient at one time to last a week or thereabouts. Further, any other kind of plain biscuit, or even mixed broken biscuits, which can often be bought very cheaply, may be used instead of the maizena, but the latter are as good as any, and much better than some other kinds, so that one is pretty safe in using these only.

EGG FOOD AND ITS MAKING.

We now come to the disputed but at present almost universal system of feeding on hard-boiled fresh egg and bread crumb, or biscuit powder. The latter is a comparatively modern addition to the egg, and has to a large extent replaced the more homely crumb of stale bread which seems to have been quite generally used by the older fanciers. And bread crumb is still the prime favourite with very many of the largest and most successful breeders of our day. That the danger from septic infection is real none need deny, but we cannot be regardless of the fact that probably ninety out of every hundred Canaries reared are brought up with the aid of hard-boiled egg. Therefore it would seem that in the present state of our knowledge we cannot do better than adhere to that course, taking care to use all the safeguards available to avert the risks of infection.

It is almost needless to point out that there exists here a fine field for the breeder of an experimental turn of mind, who might utilise the opportunity of discovering some plan of feeding that possesses all the advantages of egg-food (but in which egg finds no place) and is equally within the range of every one's abilities to procure and prepare. It should also be as readily partaken of by the bird; this is an important point to consider. The fancier who accomplishes this will not only do good to his generation, but will confer a great and lasting benefit on posterity.

So much of methods. It now only remains to give the proper mode of preparing egg-food for use, and to point out the principal dangers connected with its use. First boil the eggs for ten minutes—a few minutes extra does not matter; yet, although some fanciers say boil them twenty minutes no real advantage is gained—remove them from the water and lay them aside unbroken until quite cold, which may require an hour and a half or two hours, as the yolk retains heat after the shell feels cold. The practice of putting the eggs in cold water when removing them from that in which they have been boiled is not to be recommended, as it causes moisture to be deposited in the egg, which may, perhaps, diminish its keeping qualities. If one is pressed for time in the morning, one should boil the eggs required for the morning feed before retiring at night, and lay them aside unbroken, when they would be quite ready for use when one arises. Hard-boiled eggs (when the shell is uncracked) keep good for a considerable time.

Break open the eggs and remove the yolks, and, together with a little dry powdered biscuit, place them in the egg sieve and press all through the sieve into a basin with the back of a spoon. Stir it then with a fork, and if not sufficiently granulated add a little more dry biscuit powder, and repeat the process of pressing it through the sieve. Stir it in the basin with a fork until it is all a finely granulated mass. Then grate about twice its bulk of household bread about two days old, by turning the egg sieve over and rubbing the bread through. Of course this is supposing that one has a combined egg sieve and bread grater in use; failing this one must requisition an ordinary grater such as is commonly used in culinary operations. But providing the bread is in the proper degree of staleness these articles are not altogether indispensable as the bread can be rubbed into crumbs between the fingers just as well as with a grater. Having made a sufficient mass of bread crumb, add it to the egg in the basin and again thoroughly mix and blend all together with the fork. Do not touch the egg with the fingers, nor try to mix the ingredients by rubbing them through the fingers, as it tends to make the egg sodden and sticky. A fork is by far the best and simplest implement for mixing purposes. One now has a good wholesome soft food ready to serve out to the birds.

Some fanciers add a sprinkling of maw seed, sugar, rice powder, crushed linseed, and other things just to suit their individual fancy, or to try to induce the birds to eat more of the soft food in the hope that they will in turn "feed" more of it in due course to the young. Such a plan will succeed fairly well with some few hens who are not the best of "feeders," and require the egg-food made "tasty" (or to suit their palate) in order to induce them to partake of it freely; but with good feeding hens the simple egg and bread crumb mixture is quite the best until the young are at least five days old, when a little soaked rape seed may be added, and the proportion be gradually increased from day to day until it forms about one-third of the bulk, beyond which limit it should not go.

When biscuit powder is used instead of bread crumb, one

of the small mills which may be adjusted either to crack hemp or crush biscuits to powder will be useful. If one has to cater for many birds it may be looked upon as a necessity, as the crushing of biscuits and seeds will make quite a considerable inroad upon one's spare time unless this mechanical aid is available.

Having now gone into the details of several methods of providing food for rearing the young, I wish it to be understood that every reference to "egg-food" in these articles (unless specially mentioned to the contrary) will refer to either egg-food made with bread crumb or powdered biscuit. The use of biscuit powder in place of bread crumb is so general that it would be difficult to discriminate between the two, and perhaps, after all, there is little to choose between them. Nevertheless, I should at all times prefer crumb of good household bread.

YOLK, OR BOTH YOLK AND WHITE?

Before going back to the birds, one other point in connection with egg-food may be conveniently mentioned in this place. It is as to whether only the yolks of the eggs, or both yolks and whites should be used in making the egg-food. As with practically every other point, opinions on this matter differ considerably. Some breeders use the white as well as the yolk with very satisfactory results, whilst others find but indifferent success from this method.

It is not improbable that this lack of success may be to some extent due to the fact that the whites are not so easily broken up and granulated, so that unless the food is carefully prepared and more time spent over the mixing it is never so well blended together as when only the yolks are used. This is only an off-hand theory as to the reason why some succeed whilst others (partly at least) fail when using the same food.

My own opinion, however, is that, providing due care is exercised to see that the whites are well granulated and thoroughly blended with the food, it is perfectly safe to use them after the young are from five days to a week old. For the greater part of the first week it is quite the best to use the yolks only (and throw away the whites if no other use can be found for them), but after that time such "waste" is by no means necessary.

It will be noticed that in the detailed instructions about the mixing of egg-food, no mention is made of the addition of any kind of moistening fluid. Lest this point should be misunderstood it may be advisable to say here that (except, perhaps, in some special circumstances) no such addition is necessary. There is sufficient natural moisture in the egg and bread when blended together to bring it to a very nice degree of "crumbiness" for the birds. When ready to give to the birds the egg-food should contain no superfluous moisture that can be detected by the eye; and if a small quantity be pressed together it should, immediately it is touched, readily fall into a mass of loose crumbs again.

CHAPTER X

AT CLOSE OF INCUBATION

We may now return to the birds, and suppose that they are nearing the completion of incubation. It will have been observed that the question of testing the eggs after the first few days of incubation has been ignored. This omission has been intentional, because the new beginner will be better advised to avoid as far as possible any interference with the nest or eggs; and in any case it is doubtful whether the practice of testing the eggs is of much real utility. From the twelfth to the fourteenth day, as already intimated, the bath should be freely supplied to sitting hens if the weather is at all warm or dry.

In extreme cases it is also a good plan to immerse the eggs for a few seconds in a cupful of lukewarm water on the twelfth and thirteenth days. The object is that the moisture may help to soften the shell and its inner membrane, and thus render it easier for the chicks to release themselves. The method, however, is scarcely necessary with the first round of nests, as the atmosphere is generally charged with moisture at this time, and the bath given as indicated is quite sufficient to meet all needs if the hen bathes at all.

If all has gone well, the breeder's anxiety may be brought up to concert pitch on the evening of the thirteenth day by hearing faint "chips" if he listens awhile near the cage. In the afternoon he should give the birds either a very small piece of bread dipped in milk, or about half a teaspoonful of egg-food. Before retiring at night all that remains over of this food should be removed, and the pans washed. And then one may take a peep into the nest to see if any young are hatched. If there is no sign of the eggs hatching do not interfere with them yet. Let the hen return to them, and give another half-teaspoonful of egg-food in the egg drawer for the birds' use next morning. On the other hand, if the eggs appear to be hatching it will be better to give no egg-food at all that night, but be up betimes next morning, and when preparing the usual egg-food give this pair of birds half a teaspoonful of pure yolk of egg without any admixture of bread crumb or biscuit.

When this morning food is given another peep may be taken into the nest to see if the birds are hatched or coming out all right. If such is the case, do not commence to overload the cage with all manner of foods and dainties. Let well alone for the time, and remember that Nature has provided a food for the first hours of the chicks' lives, and that they do not require to be fed during this time; therefore, there is no cause for anxiety if the hen does not commence feeding them at once. Half a teaspoonful of egg-food will be amply sufficient until the afternoon, even with a full brood of four or five young, when a fresh supply similar in quantity and quality to that given in the morning should be provided.

Next morning the first food given should be mixed in the proportion of two parts yolk of egg to one part of bread crumb, and in the afternoon the proportion of bread crumb may be increased to one half of the bulk. On the third morning and thenceforward the usual egg-food, consisting of one part of egg to two parts of bread crumb should be given.

TESTING EGGS.

Of course, all this is written on the supposition that the beginner's lines have fallen in pleasant places; that the ideal has happened, and his dreams been realised to the full. But in actual practice things do not always run along so smoothly. It may happen that the thirteenth day has passed without the remotest "chip" from an unborn chick falling on the listener's ear, and the fourteenth morning may as dismally fail to show any sign of an egg "pipping" or "chipping" as the first visible sign of hatching is variously called.

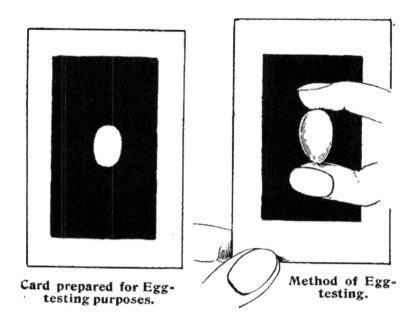

Card prepared for Egg-testing purposes.

Method of Egg-testing.

In the latter case it is as well to test the eggs for fertility. The simplest and surest way for the novice to do this is to get a piece of card-board—a postcard will answer admirably. Paste a piece of black paper (dark brown would do at a pinch) on one side of it, then cut a small oval space rather smaller than the outline of an egg out of the centre of it with a sharp penknife, and you have all you really need to test them with.

To use, take the card in the left thumb and forefinger, holding it so that the black side will be towards the eye when it is held up. Now take one of the eggs in the thumb and forefinger of the right hand, and, going to a window where there is a good light, hold the card up in front of the eye, hold the egg in front of the hole close to the card, and look through the egg towards the light. If the egg appears transparent it may be rejected at once; it is "clear," or unfertile. If it appears streaky and cloudy (semi-transparent), with darker blotches here and there, it is "addled," that is, it was fertile, but the germ from some cause has failed to develop, and died in the early days of incubation. This egg also may be discarded without more ado.

HATCHING DIFFICULTIES.

But if eggs appear dark and opaque they will contain a chick. These should be immersed for a few seconds in warm water, as mentioned above, and be returned to the nest until mid-day, and if there is then still no sign of "pipping," the immersion may be repeated. By holding the egg close to the ear one can almost always hear the movements, or "chip, chip," of the chick, and after some experience be able to judge from these indications whether the chick is strong or feeble. It is too early, however, to attempt any other interference yet. The dipping may be repeated again at night if there is still no sign of the shell "chipping" and the chick can be heard within.

Next morning if they remain in the same condition, a

small hole may be made in the large end of the egg with a bit of pointed wood, or the blunt end of a needle. An hour or two later, if no further progress is seen, the hole may be very carefully extended in the direction in which the chick's beak is seen to lie, until the beak is gradually released. Again return the egg to the nest for an hour or two to give the chick a chance of freeing itself. If it has made no progress by night, and the chick still seems to be tolerably lively, a little more of the loose shell may be gently removed from around the top, when, if fairly dry and properly developed, the chick may drop out into the hand. In this case hold it in the palm of one hand, cover it with the, other hand, and hold the hands at a little distance from the fire, and now and again breathe through the thumbs on to the bird. After a few minutes of this treatment place it in the nest and leave it to the care of the hen.

So far I have been describing an extreme case of difficult hatching. Needless to say, all the manipulations described require the most delicate handling and nicety of touch. The least clumsiness will generally prove fatal to the chick, and in the great majority of cases a similar result is to be expected if any bleeding is caused by the manipulations. Even if the young bird is got out safely without bleeding, one must not expect too much of it. They are given the only chance that was available for them to make a fight for life, but the fact remains that a large proportion of them only survive for a few days.

In a more modified form of the trouble the eggs will be "pipped" on the evening of the thirteenth or the morning of the fourteenth day, and will make no further progress towards hatching. In the evening of the fourteenth day these eggs should be dipped in warm water, as already mentioned for others, except that in these cases the eggs should be held in the thumb and forefinger with the "pipped" part uppermost, and the water should not be allowed to get up to the "pipping." After removing them from the water, and wiping the water from the shell very gently, ease the shell around the beak. If the inner membrane appears nice and dry (somewhat like a bit of tissue paper), one may gently loosen the shell a little way round on each side of the beak, so that it will require but little effort on the part of the bird to push off the top of the shell, and thus break its way out by its own efforts. Unless it is a really bad case, these chicks should be out and dry next morning.

DEAD IN SHELL, &C.

Many other cases may occur where the chicks are found dead in the shell. The fact will soon be discovered when the egg is opened a little, intentionally, to assist the chick, as a little close watching will reveal the movements of the chick, although they may be but very slight at first, if it is really alive. The cause of the young being dead in the shell is too obscure to be more than speculated upon. It may be due to prolonged cold caused by the eggs not being properly covered by the hen, or by the hen staying off the nest too long, or by natural weakness in the embryo Thunder, sudden noises and jars, such as banging a door to close it, are often accounted to blame for young dead in shell, but it is extremely doubtful whether these things have any effect at all one way or the other.

In some rare cases, when the eggs are submitted to the "light" test, they will be found very transparent, save for a small patch in the small end of the egg, which is dark and opaque. On opening these eggs it will be found that the yolk and white have completely dried up and shrunk into the small end of the shell, where the yolk lies in a tiny hardened dry mass still retaining its original colour. These eggs were probably "clear" or unfertile in the first instance, with, perhaps, defective shells of a too porous nature, which allowed the moisture to pass off too rapidly; which, of course, is all a matter of speculation again.

Before finally leaving the subject of hatching, a few words of advice may be given. Always restrict any interference to the large end of the egg, and never in any case break or damage the smaller end. Never be in a hurry to assist the birds out of the shells, and make it a point always to leave the parent birds as much to themselves as possible at this stage of the proceedings. Remember that premature interference is apt to be infinitely worse in the result than that which is a little delayed. A man's fingers are at the very best but clumsy instruments to manipulate so delicate a structure as a bird's egg and its imprisoned chick. The average working man, whose sense of touch is but too often dulled by daily toil, is in even a worse plight; so that he, at least, should always endeavour to get the assistance of a careful, steady-nerved feminine friend to perform the operations for assisting the young to hatch which have been described. To sum up, any attempt at all to assist the hatching process (except the simple dipping at intervals in warm water) is to be deprecated, and, as already stated, when such assistance is attempted one must not be over sanguine as to the results.

CHAPTER XI

FEEDING THE YOUNG CANARIES.

When the hatching process is completed one should begin to supply egg-food to each pair as occasion requires (as mentioned in detail when dealing with the brood that hatches out without trouble or assistance), beginning with pure egg yolk, and gradually bringing them on to the ordinary egg-food by the third day. From the fourteenth day until the young are three days old the bath should be withheld, unless given for some particular purpose to be named hereafter. In the meantime, if all goes well and the hen feeds the young satisfactorily, adhere to simple methods only.

For the first three days let the usual seed diet and egg-food suffice. Give the latter in small quantities, and give a freshly prepared supply, whenever possible, at least three times each day. Do not try to economise by mixing any that may be left over with the freshly made supply. This is certainly the very worst kind of false economy. Throw away all that is left, and wash out the egg drawer before giving the fresh supply.

For the first two or three days half a teaspoonful at each meal will be sufficient; but one must use his own discretion, and not adhere to any hard and fast rule as to quantities. Some birds consume a far greater amount of egg-food than others, and it is a safe plan to endeavour to regulate the supply so that the quantity given is just cleared up before the time to give a fresh supply. It is not really difficult to manage this, by noting the condition of the egg drawer for the first few days, and increasing or diminishing the supply as seems necessary.

When this plan is properly carried out the birds are keener to feed than when surfeited by having an unlimited supply of egg-food always before them; they will nearly always set to work to feed the young as soon as each fresh supply is given. The method certainly demands strict regularity in the times of feeding, but as this should be a cardinal virtue with every breeder, it should be no real obstacle; and the advantages gained by the method are very great.

WHEN ALL GOES WELL.

If all continues to go on well, and the hen feeds the young satisfactorily, give her a bath on the third day after hatching, and continue it daily afterwards. Begin also to give a little green food, commencing with a small leaf of lettuce, or spray of watercress or chickweed, and gradually increasing the quantity given from day to day until what is considered a fair allowance is reached.

The amount of egg-food must also be gradually increased as the needs of the growing brood become greater, always endeavouring to keep it within the limits already pointed out, and giving it fresh as often as is convenient. To digress for a moment, in saying this one must not imagine that by mixing a sufficient quantity of food in the morning to last through the day, and serving it out in small quantities at intervals, one is properly carrying out the principle of giving fresh food two or three times a day. This is by no means the case, and simply amounts to giving fresh food once, a day, and no oftener. To properly carry out the principle, only sufficient food should be prepared each time to supply the needs of the birds at each serving, and the remainder of the eggs required for the day's supply should remain unbroken until required for immediate use. Thus, although one may save time by boiling all the eggs required for a day's use at one time, one must not try to economise further by also mixing a sufficient *bulk* of food to last a day.

After the first three days the increased demands of a healthy brood of young will soon become apparent if the parents are fulfilling their duties properly, and the supply of egg-food will soon need to be doubled and trebled. A little crushed hemp should be given in a finger drawer on the third day, and a liberal supply of this should be continued afterwards, crushing it freshly each day (a small matter when one has a hemp crusher or mill). And from the fifth day onwards a proportion of soaked rape may be added to the egg-food, as described in the chapter treating of egg-food in detail.

Under this regimen the brood should thrive and flourish apace, and be able to leave the nest from the eighteenth to the twenty-first day after hatching. In practice, however, things do not always follow this ideal path, but are all too apt to divert from the straight course at many points and land the erstwhile hopeful owner into a veritable slough of despond. Hence we may leave the normal broods to grow and thrive, and return to the beginning to follow the more troubled course of events.

THE CROOKED PATH.

From the time the young are hatched until they are quite able to take care of themselves in the nest, one should make a point of taking a glance over the cage floor every morning and night, and trying to get a glimpse of the birds' heads as they raise them when gaping in expectation of being fed, in order to see whether a chick has been dragged out of the nest, or has died within it. In the latter case it must be removed at once, before it becomes offensive.

It sometimes happens that chicks are found on the bottom of the cage, having been accidentally dragged out of the nest in the claws or among the feathers of the hen when she left it for food, and when this occurs the chick (or chicks) is almost invariably totally ignored by the parents as soon as it is out of the nest. Should the youngster still be fairly lively when found, hold it between the palms of the hands and breathe between the thumbs upon it for a few moments until it begins to feel a little warm; then gently replace it in the nest with the others.

But should the chick appear cold and lifeless, do not jump to hasty conclusions and throw it away. Place it between the palms of the hands, as before, and hold it in this position before a fire (as near the fire as can comfortably be borne by the hands), and every now and again breathe vigorously between the thumbs on to the bird. Many a chick that is apparently quite lifeless will be resuscitated by ten or fifteen minutes of this treatment. If it shows signs of life let it get thoroughly warm, and place it in the nest with the others. Next morning it will often be impossible to distinguish it from the rest of the brood.

In cases where the young are being continually dragged out of the same nest, it is a good plan to catch the hen and examine her claws to see if they are overgrown, as this is frequently the real cause of the mischief. If this appears to be the case, carefully trim the claws to a reasonable length, but be careful not to go too close to the red vein which runs down them, and which can be seen on holding the foot up to a good light, and so make the claws bleed. It must also be understood that catching the birds and performing any kind of operation is to be avoided as far as possible at this time. It is only in cases of extreme necessity that they are recommended

Another trouble that may come early in the experience of the breeder is hens that after laying and hatching satisfactorily will refuse from the first to feed the young. In some cases, particularly "with young hens who have their first brood of young, it appears to arise from sheer nervousness, and keeping the hen as quiet and secluded as possible for a few days will often have a good result. Frequently, however, with such hens the first brood is lost, but they should be given another chance, and with future broods will often make very good parents.

SWEATING HENS CONSIDERED.

Having now considered that type of hen which does not really commence to perform her maternal duties, we may go on to another type which is, perhaps, even more disappointing to the beginner, because her conduct fills him with high hopes at the beginning, only to dash them to the ground a few days later. This type of hen will begin to feed the young and continue feeding satisfactorily for three or four days, or, perhaps, a week, when she gets affected with the trouble popularly known as "sweating," from the fact that the plumage on the hen's breast and abdomen, and also the down on the young birds, is often damp and moist, as though with perspiration. In some cases, at least, this appearance is believed to be due partly to the unduly watery evacuations of the young—a sufficient proof that the health of the young is also at fault.

In the great majority of cases, however, where the birds were in good health and condition before starting to breed, this trouble, doubtless, arises from surfeiting the birds with too great abundance of egg-food, green stuff, and other varieties of food, as soon as the young are hatched, in the hope that the more liberal and varied the diet the better they will feed the young. This is a very mistaken idea, and although it may answer in somes special cases, when the hens require some "coaxing" in order to start them to feed, it will, in the greater number of cases, defeat its own end by upsetting the birds, coming, as it does, quite suddenly after the very plain diet which suffices (or should) during the period of incubation.

When the birds are treated as already described during

the first few days after the young are hatched the latter cause will be removed, and consequently "sweating" should be comparatively uncommon. It may not yet be sufficiently well known that a frequent cause of hens "sweating" the young is believed to be due to a non-virulent type of septic bacilli, and hence somewhat akin to septic fever. Remedy, in this case, there is none; and prevention, as previously pointed out, lies in sacrificing the use of egg as a portion of the diet.

But where this sacrifice is not made the safeguard lies in a rigid adherence to the method laid down of giving the egg-food in small quantities at frequent intervals, and preparing it quite fresh each time. Further, observing, in addition, strict cleanliness and hygiene in and about the cages; floor kept free from droopings, and every particle of stale egg-food; egg-drawer, and all food and water vessels emptied and washed perfectly clean at least once every day.

These precautions being duly carried out, one must keep a sharp look out on the birds from the first in order to see that the young are being properly fed, and at the first sign of the hen beginning to shirk her duty, give a young tender leaf of lettuce, whether it be the first or the third day after hatching, and follow it up with the salt bath as described hereafter. If she does not then continue her duties with satisfaction, follow up the course of treatment as aforenamed. If tried at the very beginning of the trouble the two items just mentioned will frequently suffice to brace up a hen and prevent her becoming a non-feeder or "sweater."

USE OF A FOSTER PARENT.

But when all the means we have, gone into for keeping a hen going at her maternal duties, including the removal of the cock, have been exhausted without success there remains the last hope of saving the young by transferring them to a foster-parent. If the young being neglected are from valuable stock there is, of course, little compunction in disposing of a nest of common stock belonging to good feeding parents, and substituting the better class young for them. As with making a new nest, it is best to make their transference in the evening, and when doing so, if the young appear weak through lack of food, place a little fresh egg-food in your own mouth to warm and moisten it, and give each youngster a cropful off the end of a quill before placing them under the foster hen.

When contemplating an exchange of this kind one should endeavour to fix on a brood of young of about the same age as, or a day or two younger than, the brood that is to replace them. If one wishes to give the common young ones a chance they may either be distributed among other hens who have small broods about the same age, or given altogether to the "sweating" hen and be partly hand-fed, in which case there is just a mere chance of the hen pulling herself together and resuming her maternal duties with tolerable satisfaction in a few days.

On the whole, however, when a hen persists in "sweating" and does not respond to such treatment as indicated above, it is a much better plan to turn her into a large flight, where she can have abundant exercise for two or three weeks before mating her again. In the interval devote your attention to bringing her into a good sound healthy condition on a plain seed diet, with daily baths and strict attention to cleanliness, and if she is in poor condition of body a little bread and milk daily instead of egg-food. On the other hand, if she seems in an overfed condition, supplement the seed diet only with a liberal allowance of green food; with an occasional small pinch of Epsom salts in the drinking water. In two or three weeks such a hen may be mated up afresh if she seems in breeding condition, with a fair chance of better success.

TEMPTING DISHES.

When all is going well the young birds will be seen to increase in size and strength from day to day, and their "vocal efforts" when requiring food, or whilst being fed, will proportionately develop. Do not, however, let anxiety prompt you to be continually interfering with the nest and looking into it. Let a glance every morning and night, just to see that the birds are all safely in the nest, be sufficient. It should not be necessary to touch the nest to accomplish this, if one watches for the birds as they rise up to be fed. Avoid all interference that is not absolutely necessary.

Another type of hen will sit comfortably on the, nest continually calling to the cock for food, but rarely passing any of what he conveys to her on to her young. Such a hen will often be roused to a sense of her duties by taking the cock away and placing him out of sight and earshot. Then she is compelled to leave the nest for food and water, which not only gives the young brood a refreshing breath of air, but the effort of procuring her own food helps to arouse the hen's instincts. When she returns to the nest of gaping young, unless she is an "incorrigible," she will be almost certain to give them at least a little bit, which will have the wholesome effect of making them beg the more vigorously for more; and then by degrees in a day or two she may perform her duties with much satisfaction.

In these cases a variety of food is also advisable, the object being to tempt the hen to feed freely herself, and thereby increase the chances of the young coming in for a greater or less share. A little green food and crushed hemp (cracked, would be a better term, as the seed should not be really "crushed," but only have the husk cracked so as to leave the kernel nearly uninjured) should be given from the first—a young lettuce leaf is pre-eminent over all other green foods in such cases as these, and will induce a hen to feed the young when nothing else will.

On the other hand, I have found dandelion to decidedly aggravate the trouble, hence one of the chief reasons why I strongly advise its rejection entirely during the breeding season. I am well aware that many whose opinions are entitled to every consideration differ from this, but since I first drew attention to the fact I know many breeders have proved the truth of it.

Now and again one will find a hen that will only feed the young on some particular food—sometimes it is green food, or it may be cracked hemp. But whatever it is, a supply of that food must be given. It is remarkable how well some hens will bring up young apparently on green food alone.

Many other plans and nostrums have been put forward from time to time to cure the "non-feeding" hen; such as placing a cube of common salt between the wires for the birds to peck at, or adding sufficient to the water for one day to make it taste slightly of the salt; or adding sufficient Epsom salts to the drinking water for a day to make it taste slightly of that drug—all of which are harmless enough to warrant a trial in very bad cases.

But little must be expected from these crude methods. The only real "cure," if such it can be called, probably lies in the proper feeding and management of the birds prior to the time the young are hatched.

Very good results may also be obtained in some cases by this simple treatment if it is begun as soon as a hen is seen to be neglecting her duties, or, rather, not beginning them. Give a small piece of bread soaked in cold milk—not boiled— fresh two or three times a day instead of the usual egg-food, and supply a saline bath. Prepare the latter by dissolving a dessertspoonful of common salt in a pint of water and give it to the bird to bathe in. If she does not seem inclined to bathe, blow a little over her from a spray, just sufficient to bedew her plumage, when she will probably enter the bath and complete her toilet.

Whether this bath possesses any really exhilarating influences for Canaries, I do not profess to say, but it certainly will often serve to brace a hen so that she is quite brisk about her maternal duties. Altogether this last-named treatment I consider far the most satisfactory.

The increase in the food supply and the inclusion of a supply of soaked rape seed (either given separately or mixed with the egg-food), from about the fifth day has already been pointed out. It cannot be too strongly impressed upon one here to take note of the egg-food, should the rape be added to it, as during fairly warm weather a very few hours will suffice to turn it sour.

A very good plan is to place a sufficient quantity of rape seed to last two or three days in a mug or basin and fill up with cold water. Each day the whole contents may be poured into a sieve, the seed returned to the vessel, and a fresh supply of water added. In this way the seed will keep perfectly sweet for some days, and if it begins to sprout, it will be no detriment whatever. It also has the advantage of being always ready for use, so that it is only necessary to ladle out the required quantity at any time with a spoon, drain off the water, and dry the seed in a towel.

CHAPTER XII

PLUCKING THE YOUNG

All may go well until the young are ten or twelve days old, by which time the quills of the future feathers should be well developed. From this time onward until the birds are quite "on their own," another trouble is likely to beset the breeder. The hens, even although feeding and brooding the young as well as one could wish, will sometimes commence to pluck out their quills or immature feathers.

This is always a serious trouble, not only on account of its baneful effect upon the growth and development of the young, but in that it is often quite impossible to cope with it. Feather plucking, as it is called, may either arise from a desire on the part of the hen to begin nesting again, or, as sometimes appears, from sheer depravity or viciousness on her part, for the trouble is nearly always confined to the hen

In the former case, provided she is a hen one knows will feed and rear her young without the cock, he should be removed (as before described), and this is usually all that is required to overcome the difficulty in these cases.

When the hen begins to pluck the quills or feathers out of the young, and yet does not appear anxious to begin nesting again, little can be done to prevent her unless the young have reached a stage when their bodies are fairly well clothed with feathers, so that they are able to do without the hen sitting over them during the greater part of the day. If the plucking becomes really serious at such a stage in the development of the young, and one has ample opportunities for transferring the young to more careful parents, this is really the best and most practical course to pursue, carrying out the exchange as aforenamed, with the exception of giving no young of any kind to the offending hen.

RED MITES AND PLUCKING.

One thing we may mention before going further. At the very commencement of plucking always examine the nest carefully to see if mites are at the root of the mischief. If a wooden box is used, unhang it, and examine the back and the part of the cage against which it hangs, for colonies of red mite. If they are found to be the cause the remedy is sufficiently obvious.

Make a new nest in a clean box or pan, as described in detail in an early article, dusting the bottom of the box freely with pyrethrum powder before putting in the hair; also dust a little around the sides after the nest is made, and place the young birds in the clean nest.

As soon as the exchange is made burn the infested nest, and plunge the box or pan into boiling water for a minute or two. Above all, do not make the mistake of transferring the birds to the clean nest, and then allowing the infested nest to stand about in the room whilst some other task is being done, thus allowing a goodly number of its tenants to quit, and locate themselves elsewhere in the room. After giving a clean nest it will be advantageous to give the hen a few baths in which a little quassia extract has been dissolved.

Should the plucking commence when the feathers of the young are well through the quills so that they do not require the constant brooding of the hen, the nest box may be removed and placed in a nursery cage (from which the perches have been removed) during the greater part of the day. The nursery cage, which is simply a small open wire cage fitted with hooks for hanging it on to the front of the breeding cage, is then hung in position on the front of the breeding cage so that the old birds can just comfortably reach the young through the wires when they gape for food, but cannot easily reach them when they are lying snugly in the bottom of the nest.

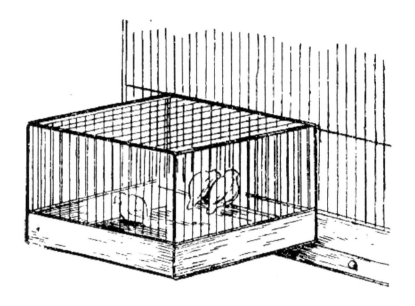

Young Birds in Nursery Cage.

Then a small piece of partly ravelled string may be tied to a wire of the breeding cage in some place a little away from the part occupied by the nursery; or a few short pieces of soft hay may be thrown inside for the hen to amuse herself with. This will often counteract the propensity to pluck the feathers out of the young.

Another plan when plucking occurs at a later stage, when the young are able to get on the side of the nest, or, perhaps, have left the nest altogether, and the cock has been left with the hen during hatching and rearing, if she does not appear bent on nesting again at once, and the cock is a good feeder, is to take the hen away and leave the cock to finish rearing the young. If double breeding cages are used it is only necessary to shut off the hen by herself in one compartment until the young are old enough for the process to be reversed—i.e., to shut the young off by themselves and leave both parents together in the other compartment, when they may begin nesting again as soon as they feel so disposed, and will still go on feeding through the wired part of the partition.

A WATCHFUL EYE.

But even when all goes along smoothly and none of the foregoing troubles arise, one still needs to keep a watchful eye over the birds and their surroundings, besides adhering to the routine work of supplying fresh food regularly, and at as frequent intervals as can be made to fit in with one's ordinary avocation, keeping the cages and all appliances scrupulously clean and free from everything in the shape of stale, sour, or decaying scraps of food, and seeing that insect pests make no headway.

This latter is an important item, and even though one should fail to discover a single mite in the cages, it is always the safest plan to make it a point to touch the corners of the cages inside, the joints of the doors, the ends of the perches, and the grooves in which the partition slides with a brush dipped in fir-tree oil or some other insecticide at each weekly cleaning. Occasionally the back of the nest box, if a wooden one, or the bottom if an earthenware pan, may be brushed over with the same liquid. The importance of persevering with these precautions will be obvious to all who have had the misfortune of witnessing the alarming increase of the red mite pest during warm weather once they put in an appearance, and it is only strict attention to preventive methods as first indicated that will prevent their appearance.

The nest is often a breeding ground for mites, and as it also apt to get soiled by the birds and present an unsightly appearance when the young are about a fortnight old, it should be replaced by a new nest in a clean pan about this time, the soiled nest being burnt at once, and the box or pan dealt with in the same manner as an insect-infested nest.

CHAPTER XIII

GOOD-BYE TO THE NEST.

The young birds will usually be able to leave the nest when a little over three weeks old. No hard and fast rule can be laid down as to the exact time they should be out of the nest. So much naturally depends upon the circumstances of each particular case as regards the number of the brood, the strength or otherwise of the birds, and whether the parents have been good or bad feeders, and to some little extent the state of the weather. But from twenty-one to twenty-eight days may be regarded as the period when the birds are likely to leave the nest.

A small brood of two or three young, well-cared for by good feeding parents, will frequently leave the nest at twenty-one days old, particularly when the weather has been generally favourable, whereas another brood, perhaps of four or five young, only indifferently fed by the old birds, may remain in the nest until twenty-eight or even thirty days old. But a brood of good, strong, healthy birds, properly fed and cared for, will almost certainly be on the perches on the twenty-fourth or twenty-fifth day after hatching.

Here, however, is another point where the young beginner is apt to go wrong. At about three weeks old he sees the young birds in the nest so large and plump that they appear to fill the nest pan, and to be almost as densely clothed on their bodies as their parents, and he cannot restrain his anxiety to see them on the perches, and is perhaps, frequently having a look in to see if they are still in the nest. At this period also, the young are very shy and restless, and very often the slightest disturbance will cause a little panic amongst them, and away they go floundering over the side of the nest on to the floor of the cage, where they are often destined to remain until they are able to balance themselves on the perches, as it is rarely that they can be induced to stay in the nest once they leave it after reaching this age. It goes without saying that this is a thing to be strictly avoided.

On the contrary, it is advisable to endeavour to keep the young in the nest as long as possible, and the only means to this end is to avoid all interference with the nest when the birds are getting nicely fledged, to keep them quite quiet, and go quietly about the daily task of cleaning and feeding the birds, being especially careful to avoid any rapid movement or sudden noise or jar about the cages containing young in this stage of development. The breeder need have no fear of the young staying in the nest longer than is good for them, as their natural desires all lie in the reverse direction, and as soon as they are really able to get about the perches, nothing will induce them to remain in the nest.

MARKING THE YOUNG.

If one is breeding on pedigree lines—a system, by the way, which may be carried out with the very commonest as well as the highest class of stock, and is equally useful in striving to obtain any given point which may be required in the commonest birds—such, for example, as in producing a race of Sib-bred birds from common stock for use in light Mule breeding—it will be necessary to mark the young birds before they are ready to leave the nest. This is usually done by placing a numbered ring on the leg of each bird, the history of the bird's breeding being then entered in a book kept for the purpose, against a number tallying with the number on the ring which the bird wears.

This marking process is best carried out at the same time as the young are provided with a clean nest, as it will save disturbing the birds to do it on a separate occasion. It will also be found a fair average time to put on the rings, as there is a right and a wrong time for the marking to be done. Thus, if the rings are put on too early, before the birds' feet have attained sufficient size to prevent them dropping off, there is a great risk of the rings slipping off again, whilst, on the other hand, if the ringing is delayed too long there may be a difficulty in getting the ring over the foot, and a certain amount of risk of dislocating the bird's hind toe.

Ringing is quite a simple matter when performed in the right way. Begin by placing the requisite number of rings in a convenient position on the table, and if changing the nests at the same time place the new nest to the right of the rings, and bring the nest of birds and set it down a little to the left. Now take a bird in the left hand, holding it with its head towards the wrist and the second, third, and fourth fingers folded down over the shoulders and wing; then draw its leg out with the thumb and forefinger of the right hand, lay the hind toe back against the leg, and grasp the leg and hind claw together between the tips of the left thumb and forefinger. Now pick up a ring, pass the three front toes through it all together, and push it upwards over the leg and hind toe, until it is past the end of the hind toe, when the toe may be allowed to fall into its proper position, and the ring will remain on the leg and be prevented dropping off by the position of the toes.

The bird is then placed in the clean nest and the process repeated with all the others in rotation. If the birds are very young, or very small when the rings are put on, it will be advisable to examine the legs a day or two later in order to make sure that none of the rings have slipped off into the nest.

WHEN OUT OF THE NEST.

When the young have finally left the nest they should be allowed to remain with their parents as long as the latter treat them kindly, and the hen shows no signs of beginning to nest again. No advantage will be gained by taking the young away as soon as they appear able to do for themselves; but the reverse often holds good. And it should be always borne in mind that even when the young appear to crack seed quite easily it is often several days longer before they are quite able to supply all their own wants. It is, therefore, much the best plan to err on the side of leaving them with their parents a few days too long rather than run the risk of separating them too early.

In all ordinary cases let the behaviour of the hen be your guide in the matter, as the promptings of nature generally result in a more or less severe onslaught upon the young by the hen when she is really anxious to begin nesting again. Then the young must be placed either on the other side of the wired partition, if a double breeding cage, or in a nursery cage fitted with a perch in such a position that when the nursery is hung on to the breeding cage and the young birds are on the perch, they will be in a convenient position for the cock to feed through the wires.

At this time the nursery cage must also be kept supplied with food, and the floor be nicely sanded. For food give a pan of the usual egg-food fresh at least twice a day, and a saucer or box full of cracked hemp, canary seed, and canary seed that has been soaked for an hour or two. These may be mixed together in the proportion of two parts dry canary seed, to one part each of hemp and soaked canary.

After a day or two, when the birds are seen to help themselves freely from the food vessels, and the quantity of seed husks in the nursery shows that they are cracking seeds quite freely, the proportion of hemp and soaked seed should be gradually diminished until the birds are wholly on a diet of dry canary seed. When placed in the nursery no water need be given for the first day or two except for an hour or so morning and evening, and no green food of any kind should be given at this stage.

By the time the young are ready to wean on to a diet of dry seeds they should be very active and lusty, and should be transferred from the nursery cage to one of a fair size in which they may remain for a few days preparatory to being finally transferred to a large flight cage, or aviary, where they may remain to grow and thrive until the moulting season is at hand, or until next spring if the birds are only required for stock purposes

The flight cage, it may be here remarked, is simply an enlarged or elongated edition of the breeding cage in which the birds are able to take short flights to get from one perch to another. For this reason it will be obvious that a flight cage should not be overcrowded with perches, which should be sufficiently far apart to compel the, birds to make some slight efforts with their wings in getting from perch to perch. Where space is limited the double breeding cage with the middle partition removed will make a tolerable flight cage after the breeding season is over.

CERTAIN EXCEPTIONS.

There are also certain exceptions to the practice of keep-the young all together which must be mentioned here. This occurs when the birds are of the Lizard variety—we should have instanced the London Fancy, too, did not that breed seem quite so extinct—which are sometimes much addicted to plucking each other's plumage, and as the birds are practically ruined for show purposes after losing their first wing and tail feathers the risk is too great to cage them together if they show the slightest tendency to contract the habit. In such cases the only safe plan is to cage them separately, or at most in couples.

This tendency to pluck each other is apt to occur in all varieties, and a few short pieces of soft hay, or seedy heads of grass, strewn occasionally on the floor of the flight cage is a good preventative, as it finds some amusement for the birds and thus draws their attention from each other's plumage.

When the birds are first removed from the nursery cage a close watch must be kept over them for a day or two in order to be sure they are quite able to care for themselves. If they go about with a depressing, miserable "cheep, cheep," and appear next morning looking thick and ruffled, and still uttering occasionally the same mournful note, the probability is that they are not yet able to feed themselves properly, and no time should be lost in returning these particular birds to the nursery and giving the cock a little fresh choice food, when he will doubtless give the hungry little ones a good feed. Leave them there for an hour or two, and return them for a similar period each day for the next day or two.

WHEN FEEDING THEMSELVES.

As soon as the young are well on a diet of dry canary seed, the supply of egg-food should be gradually diminished, and replaced by an occasional supply of bread and milk. Green food must also be discontinued as soon as the young are placed in the nursery, and no more need be given to the young until the half-ripened green seed stalks of plantain—the so-called rats' tails—are available, when these may be given freely with advantage. In the interval an occasional treat with soaked rape seed, prepared as already described for the old birds, may supply the place of green food. But let the staple diet consist of good sound canary, with just a sprinkling of rape now and again, and a little bread and milk two or three times a week.

Keep the cage floor scrupulously clean and nicely sanded with a coarse, gritty sand, and occasionally throw in a few short white oats. But do not over-do the latter item, and always use discretion in giving them, as with some birds they are apt to upset the digestive system, and when this is the case it goes without saying that they are better withheld. They are a valuable item of food, however, for the larger varieties of Canary, when they can be used without any bad effect, as they assist materially in building up that frame and muscle which is a very essential feature of the make-up of these varieties. The remarks just made about green food, let me say, are intended to apply only to the young birds.

CHAPTER XIV

CONCERNING THE PARENTS

Here we may leave the young for a short time in order to give a few valedictory remarks on the old birds and their general management. When the parents are about going to nest the second time the nest-box or pan should be removed; the place where it has hung against the cage be brushed over with the liquid mite destroyer; a perfectly clean and disinfected box or pan hung in place; the piece of cuttlefish thrown away if at all soiled and a fresh piece substituted; and new nesting material supplied.

In short, clear out everything that has been used for the rearing of the first brood, and supply a fresh clean set of materials. Burn, at once, all that is not capable of being effectually disinfected by boiling—the easiest of all really effectual methods which are quite within the reach and power of everybody to perform. Never try to economise by using the same material for two nests in succession. It is often an extremely costly method of management in the end.

If a fairly large flake of cuttlefish is left and it is only slightly soiled, the outer crust should be cut off until what remains is quite clean, when it might be, used over again. But even in this matter we prefer to use small pieces in the first instance, and burn what is left when the birds are ready to go to nest again.

Provided the first brood are quite "on their own" when the parents commence nesting again, the daily supply of egg-food must not be kept up. This should be discontinued as soon as the young are quite able to do for themselves, dropping it gradually for the first few days, so that the change is not too sudden. The unlimited supply of hemp, the soaked rape, and all the other items which were supplied for the rearing of the young must also be dropped, so that in about a week after the young are taken away the parents are again on the diet of plain seeds and green food—dandelion excepted—which was the regimen when first going to nest.

As with the young, an occasional tit-bit of bread and milk may very advantageously take the place of egg-food. Care must be taken, however, that it does not become sour It will be best at this time to scald the bread with boiling milk, as it will not then go sour so quickly, and the heat of the weather being so much greater for the second broods all these foods are rendered proportionately more risky to use unless extra vigilance is exercised to keep them fresh and sweet. With these little differences the plan of management of the old birds for the second or third broods will be simply a repetition of the details already given for the first brood.

Although we have mentioned a third brood, it should not be taken to imply that this number of broods should be taken from each pair of birds. There will arise many cases when three broods may be safely taken from a pair of birds: such as one mating up the birds too early and getting a clutch of unfertile eggs in consequence, or when a brood is lost quite young. In either case if the pair of birds are healthy and vigorous and show a desire to nest again immediately, it will be safe enough to allow them to have a third brood, and no harm will result. But when the first and second broods are reared it will, as a rule, be far more satisfactory to break up the breeding pairs when the second brood is removed. In any case, from the middle to the end of June should be the latest for allowing a pair to go to nest again.

HOT WEATHER MANAGEMENT CONSIDERED.

In the general management, which will apply equally to old and young birds, the chief differences will be such as are mainly due to the increased normal temperature. The weather will frequently have grown quite hot by the time the second brood is about due to hatch, and in anticipation of this event the bath should be used more freely all through the period of incubation. Indeed, the bath will have to be used more freely throughout, and once or twice a week should have a few quassia chips soaked in it, or a few drops of extract of quassia added thereto.

The periodical dressing of the cages with mite destroyer will also need to be performed twice a week, and the water vessels will need regular attention at least once every day. It is not sufficient to just empty out what is left and fill up again. The vessels must be well rinsed every time they are emptied before refilling, and well washed once a week.

DURING OPPRESSIVE HEAT.

The ventilation will also need careful attention when the weather becomes warm. Open windows should be the order of the day—and of the night, too, if it can be arranged with safety during hot, sultry weather. Providing means are adopted to prevent a direct rush of air into the cages in the shape of draughts, one cannot be too liberal in the supply of fresh air.

One word of caution may not be out of place here. Do not imagine that a sweet fragrant smelling room which is due to a liberal use of disinfectants or deodorisers is hygienically safe if fresh pure air is not freely admitted. Disinfectants are very valuable in their proper place, but will never supply the place of fresh air. During the summer a shallow dish filled with a dark crimson solution of permanganate of potash kept exposed in the room and changed as often as the fluid changes to a dirty brown colour has a very refreshing effect, but do not imagine that it is going to convert a hot-bed of disease into a sanatorium.

When the heat is oppressive and the birds appear fagged by it, a sheet or a large towel or two wrung out in cold water and hung across the room to dry will have an immediate effect in reducing the temperature, which may be kept down to a comfortable degree as long as seems necessary by wetting the sheet again and again as it becomes dry.

It is during such conditions of weather as we have just been describing that the seeds of septic fever are apt to be sown broadcast amongst the birds by a lax method of preparing and giving the egg-food. It cannot be gainsaid that the risk of contracting this malady is always present; but at this season, and under such conditions as just described, when sufficient egg-food is given in the morning to last until night, and, perhaps, the egg drawers only imperfectly cleaned when renewing the supply, the risk becomes very grave.

It may, however, be reduced to a minimum by preparing only sufficient egg-food for immediate use, as mentioned in an early part of this book; by keeping it rather on the side of dryness than unnecessary moisture (never add water to it); and giving it fresh as often as possible, three or four times a day if it can be managed. The working man fancier would find the aid of the feminine "powers that be" of great value in performing this task for him. It is, all too often, an impossible one for him to perform himself on account of the daily toil taking him from home during the greater part of the day.

CHAPTER XV

WHEN WEANED

We may now return to the young whom we left in the flight or separate cages doing well for themselves. After being properly weaned off the soft food they should be got on to a diet of plain canary seed. This should form the staple diet until the birds are about to drop into moult, and it should be bright, clean, and sweet. Avoid all dusty, musty, inferior samples.

Egg-food for the time being may very advantageously be replaced by a saucer of bread and milk (all the superfluous milk should be drained away) two or three times a week and on the alternating days a small pinch each of a mixture of about equal parts of hemp, rape, maw, and oats, or soaked rape. Let them have access to clean coarse, gritty sand, and keep a piece of cuttlefish in the cage.

Green food has already been dealt with. But when the nasturtiums begin to bloom a few of the blooms may be thrown into the flight. They will do no harm, and if the birds acquire a liking for them they may be given freely when the moult is coming on, and will add depth and tone to the bird's colour of that soft and delicate hue which will be recognised on the show bench as "natural colour."

Baths should be supplied freely, as with the old birds, but at all times one should use discretion in this matter. Thus, if a bird is weak and susceptible to cold, as is sometimes shown by the bird sitting huddled up on the perch after bathing instead of hustling about and drying itself, the bath should certainly be withheld whenever there is a sudden drop in the normal temperature and the air feels chilly. Such a bird as we have in mind will often have its plumage quite damp an hour after it has bathed, and even in the summer when the normal temperature has suddenly fallen ten, fifteen, or twenty degrees, as it often does, and there is for the time a feeling of chilliness in the air, these birds run a more or less serious risk of contracting inflammation.

It is in such cases as these that the individual fancier would do well to exercise his own discretion, independently of all dogmas laid down in the hard and fast rules of what one might term cut and dried systems of bird breeding.

A GREAT DISAPPOINTMENT.

Providing the mode of treatment we have outlined has

been adhered to, and proper attention paid to cleanliness in everything connected with the hobby, ventilation, and general hygiene, the young birds should not, so to speak, look behind them once they are "well on seed"—which is the apt phrase of the fancier for describing the time when the birds are properly weaned off soft food and able to support themselves on the usual staple diet of seeds.

But there very frequently comes another great disappointment when the birds reach about six, eight, or ten weeks old. Then they often begin to drop off in numbers after perhaps a week's illness, during which time they waste away to mere skeletons of skin and bone. When birds begin to die off in numbers at this season it is always well to suspect septic fever and take the necessary steps to assure oneself whether this is the real cause, meanwhile adopting precautionary measures as far as possible to prevent it spreading.

But when the deaths are limited to the young birds about the ages mentioned above, and the adult stock and the young that are still with them continue to do well and keep healthy, it is pretty strong evidence against the theory of septic fever, which more usually breaks out amongst the adult stock when the vital resistance is lowered by breeding, and, consequently, these birds and the young that are with them are the first to begin to die off.

When septic fever is not the cause of the young birds'

troubles it is in all probability due to digestive derangements caused by improper feeding and management generally. It is often ascribed to the giving of green food to the young birds before the moult, and there is just so much truth in this assumption as that a free supply of varied greenstuffs carelessly thrown to the birds at intervals is just as likely as anything to upset the digestive system and help to bring about the more serious complications that follow. We have already indicated what kind of green food might safely be given.

As regards the treatment of the birds suffering from these dietetic indiscretions nothing short of rational feeding and management will be of much service. If the birds appear very weak do not put them on a fresh diet of seeds too suddenly. Give them firstly half a teaspoonful of fluid magnesia and six drops of lemon juice in each ounce of drinking water until the bowels are freely moved, and for the first two or three days feed on bread sopped in milk and squeezed nearly dry, with about one small teaspoonful of canary seed per bird per day. Give no green food at all while the illness lasts. Continue this treatment until the birds are recovered and then bring them on to the diet mentioned above for the young birds when able to do for themselves, which should prevent any recurrence of the trouble.

To sum up, given plenty of good, plain, wholesome

food, free access to gritty sand and cuttlefish, clean, pure water, fresh pure air, space for abundant exercise, and absolute cleanliness throughout the room, cages, and all appurtenances are the fell enemies of disease and ill-health in the young, given healthy stock to begin with, and under these conditions birds will be found subject to but very few ailments.

The moult, which is usually considered a critical period in a bird's life, only becomes seriously so when the birds are kept under unhealthy conditions, or improperly fed. Under the reverse conditions, though not without a certain amount of poor health, it should not be really serious. It will begin to manifest itself when the birds are from eight to twelve weeks old, the later hatched birds dropping into moult at a younger age than those from early nests.

CHAPTER XVI

NEARING THE JOURNEY'S END

We cannot more fittingly close these articles on the elementary side of Canary breeding than by giving a few notes on the last stages, as it were, of development, seeing that the birds can scarcely be considered quite mature until the first moult is completed. In the larger varieties, at least, we are strongly inclined to place the point of maturity forward for several months after the completion of the first moult.

Another item—training—may be dealt with briefly here. Our aim has been to just lead the reader along to success in breeding and rearing Canaries, without regard to variety, colour, marking, or any fancy point whatever, so that we need scarcely deal exhaustively with this subject, which belongs essentially to the work of the practised breeder of birds for exhibition.

About the middle of July the birds will begin to show signs of dropping into moult, which is the very practical and efficient plan employed by Nature for disposing of the old, soiled, and worn plumage of birds and replacing it with new. In adult Canaries this change should be thorough and complete at the end of each summer—that is, the whole of the plumage from beak to tail should be cast off and replaced by new. In young Canaries, however, the process may be regarded as only partial, as the whole of the plumage is not changed naturally at the first moult. The tail, and the large quill feathers in the wings—also called the "flights"—are the parts that, in the natural course of events, are not cast off until the second moult. All the smaller feathers are cast off and replaced by new ones.

We say the flights and tail are not shed in the natural course of events advisedly, because it is the frequent custom of the expert colour feeder to forcibly pluck out these feathers during the time the birds are moulting. The object of this is that the new feathers may be acted upon by the colour food, as it is only during the growth of the new feathers that the colour can be materially affected by foods, and secondarily, though this is a point of minor importance, to obtain a little extra length of these feathers where it is required. Tailing and flighting, as this plucking is called, we regard as a cruel and useless practice, and one that should not be tolerated. Its only uses are those already mentioned, and surely we could well dispense with these trivial improvements for the birds' first season.

APPROACH OF THE MOULT.

The oncoming of the moult will be quickly distinguished by the effect upon the birds even before any feathers are dropped. The disastrous and fatal effects which are seen on improperly managed and weakly stock have been already dealt with. Given healthy and robust birds, rationally treated, these baneful effects are very rarely experienced. With this class of birds there is probably a feeling of drowsiness and lassitude, but not of actual illness.

At first the bird may pick over its food without eating for a day or two; then it snatches a few minutes rest on the perch at intervals during the day, rouses up, stretches its legs and wings, and appears quite itself again for a time; it settles down to roost earlier at night; then it begins picking about the bottom of its cage a good deal without any apparent object in doing so; next it will be observed frequently inspecting its plumage with a critical eye, picking at a feather here and another there, and giving itself a good shake; finally a stray feather or two will be found in the cage—an unmistakeable proof, not that the moult is about to begin, but that it has already commenced and is in progress.

By observing these symptoms from the onset the fancier soon learns to tell with great nicety when the moult will begin. Some of the symptoms detailed above, such as constant picking at the feathers, are very similar to the effects of red mite. Of course, the fancier can easily satisfy himself on this point, but taking the symptoms altogether it will not be easy to mistake the moult for attacks of red mite; besides, unless the cages are in a shocking condition with this pest, the effects of the latter will not be so noticeable during the day as for an hour or two after the birds have settled down to roost in the evening.

But supposing the fancier is able to recognise the very first indications of approaching moult, it by no means follows that he must wait until these symptoms manifest themselves before making preparation for moulting and colour-feeding the birds. If they are of good stock, and it is desired to moult them for show purposes, they should be kept in couples in proper moulting cages during this period. And it goes without saying that these cages should be thoroughly cleaned and overhauled first before the birds are drafted into them. It is sheer folly to place a bird to moult in a cage that is not spotlessly clean, otherwise the new plumage is soiled before it is fully grown.

COLOUR FEEDING.

Then as regards colour-feeding: as intimated above, it is only possible to materially improve the colours of the feathers whilst they are actually in process of formation, as it were, so that it will be easy to understand that it is absolutely essential to begin giving the colour food some time in advance of the feathers beginning to drop out. The object of this is to ensure the blood supply being well impregnated with colouring matter ready to be deposited in the tissues of the new feathers at the very source of growth. Therefore, the safest plan is to commence giving a little colour food two or three times a week about the end of June, and in the first or second week of July give a small quantity daily to all the birds. It will not be necessary to give a full average quantity at this time—a third part of the usual quantity will suffice until the birds show signs of dropping into moult, when the quantity should be gradually increased to twice as much, which will be sufficient for another week or two. It is the early-hatched young birds which should be earliest got on to the colour-food.

In purchasing colour-food one cannot be too particular in insisting upon the purity of the materials supplied. The cheapest food, if loaded with non-colouring matter or adulterants, is certain to prove dearest in the end; it is, therefore, the best policy to pay more in the beginning and insist upon having a pure article. There are many good and skilfully blended foods on the market, advertised in the columns of CAGE BIRDS, but as all must, or rather ought to, consist of practically the same elements, it would be invidious to single out any particular brand for mention.

But if the breeder wishes to procure the pure ingredients separately, and mix his own food, the following blend will serve every useful purpose, and produce practically every shade of yellow or orange by simply varying the quantity of food used—the greater the proportion of colour food employed the nearer one approaches to, a red tone, and vice versa:—

> 12 ozs. tasteless red pepper.
>
> 1 oz. best Natal pepper.
>
> 3 ozs. soft sugar.

If a decided red tone is desired the proportion may be varied as follows:—

> 12 ozs. tasteless red pepper.
>
> 2 ozs. best Natal pepper.
>
> 2 ozs. soft sugar.

In either case the ingredients should be thoroughly mixed and blended together, and kept ready for use in a glass or earthenware jar, closely corked. Many breeders mix and blend a little oil in the colour food, but in my opinion as good results are obtained without it, and the birds seem to like the food better. Still, if one prefers to use oil it is only necessary to add one ounce of best salad oil to the mixture of pepper, whilst being stirred, and continue mixing and blending until all trace of the oil seems to have disappeared.

PROCEDURE DURING COLOUR FEEDING.

To give the colour-food prepare the egg-food in the usual way, and to each small teacupful of egg-food add two heaped teaspoonfuls of the colour-food, and blend all together until the whole is one even mass of colour. Then serve it out to the birds in the same way as egg-food, giving about the same quantity. When the birds are about to begin dropping their feathers give this food regularly every day, and increase the quantity of colour-food to three, and a few days later to four teaspoonfuls to each teacupful of egg-food.

In the middle of the moult, particularly if the birds are dropping their feathers very rapidly, again increase the colour-food to five or six teaspoonfuls to the above quantity for a short time. When the birds are well past the middle of the moult the proportion of colour-food must be decreased a little at a time, and finish off with three spoonfuls to the same quantity of egg-food as given above.

The object of this decrease is to preserve an even colour all over. If a full proportion of colouring matter is given right through the moult it is easy to understand that after the majority of the body feathers have been replaced, the drain on the colour supply being more limited, a much larger proportion of colouring matter accumulates to be deposited in the feathers that remain to be shed; consequently the head and neck, which are the last parts to be moulted, will come out a hotter colour than the rest of the body if the proportion of colour-food is not decreased.

To obtain the best results it is essential to observe the strictest regularity in supplying the colour-food. It must be given every day without fail all through the moult, and for a little time after the birds appear quite fine in feather. Negligence in this respect is the cause of birds coming through the moult patchy in colour.

Do not be in too great a hurry to take the birds off colour-food, as it often happens that a great number of quills remain to be developed after the birds are apparently quite fine.

To fix the colour and make it more lasting a crystal of sulphate of iron about the size of a hemp-seed should be dissolved in the drinking water two or three days a week during the latter part of the moult, and on the following day after giving iron, add 12 drops of glycerine to the water to counteract the constipation which is apt to follow the use of iron.

CHAPTER XVII

THE FIRST STAGE OF THE MOULT.

Having now dealt at some length with the subject of colour-feeding we go on to more general aspects of the moult. After getting the birds on to the colour-food before any feathers have been cast off, as already pointed out, the birds may still be left for the present in groups in the flight and store cages. (Lest these terms should not be obvious to everyone we will digress for a moment to say that a "flight cage" is simply a large cage, which should not be overcrowded with perches, in which the birds can get abundant exercise, and are compelled to make some little use of their wings in travelling from perch to perch, whilst a "store cage" is a similar structure for keeping a number of birds together after the close of the breeding season. For all practical purposes the two terms may be regarded as synonymous.) During this interval the time may be devoted to getting the moulting cages ready for the reception of the birds.

The usual type of moulting cage is, so to speak, a kind of dwarf breeding cage, minus the usual breeding appliances, being little more than one-half the height of a breeding cage, and about the same length and depth. About half the height of the front from the floor is of wood, with wires above, and only two perches are required, both on a level with the bottom of the wires. A water vessel, seed-box, and egg drawer, are all the fitments required. It will thus be seen that only a comparatively small amount of strong light can enter the moulting cages, which is a decided advantage during the later stages of the moult of such delicately-coloured birds as Canaries, as the strongest rays of white light have a detrimental effect upon the tone of colour.

IMPORTANCE OF EXERCISE.

It is, however, most advisable to allow the birds the benefit of the extra space for exercise in the larger cages until they have commenced to cast off their feathers. Then all the most typical specimens, and such as appear likely to make birds fit for exhibition, should be drafted into the moulting cages in twos or threes. They will invariably be found to feed better in this way than when caged up separately, because the birds will take to the soft food far more freely when two or more are together than when alone.

At the same time, one must not go to the other extreme of putting too many in each cage, or quarrelling, and, perhaps, feather-plucking are apt to arise. This feather-plucking is a danger which the breeder must keep a sharp look-out for all through the moult, and if it occurs the culprits must be discovered and immediately removed and caged alone, otherwise the plucked birds will probably come out of the moult very uneven and patchy in colour, and in the case of Lizards may have their show prospects seriously damaged.

All the other birds—those that are not to be specially fed for colour (stock birds for next season's breeding), and those that are not to be colour-fed at all may be left in the large cages all through the moult, when they will doubtless derive much benefit from the extra exercise they will be able to obtain, although as a rule, the moulting season will be rather more prolonged with these birds than with those in the moulting cages.

Where space and time to give the necessary attention to the extra supply of cages exists, we should feel inclined to give preference to the plan of moulting all the birds in moulting cages for the sake of the little shortening of the moulting season that would accrue. A rapid moult is always better than a slow one, and a bird that casts its feathers "all at once," so to speak, will invariably get through its moult better and in finer condition than its fellows who are slowly dragging their way through for weeks after the former are ready to appear on the show bench if required. Certainly when the moult progresses very rapidly and the birds are in consequence very thinly clad, care must be taken to avoid cold draughts about the cages.

FRESH AIR AND BATHS.

This, of course, does not mean that fresh air must be shut out of the room; quite the contrary, you cannot at any time have too much fresh pure air, but always see that it is not accompanied by draughty cages. The simplest improvised screen of paper or curtains will often divert a current of air going direct into the stack of cages.

The bath also must be given with discretion during the middle of the moult. With birds that are particularly subject to chills, such as we noted in an earlier chapter, the bath may be withheld for a time, or failing that the water should be allowed to stand in the sun for an hour or so before being placed in the bath.

This precaution will go far to prevent birds growing imperfect feathers, particularly in the wings and tail, with narrow, dark, thread-like lines across the webs, and which, when held up to the light, are seen to be deficient in webbing where the lines exist. Such feathers are well known to every breeder and are generally believed to be due to the ravages of red mite. That this is an erroneous opinion is easily proved by the same thing occurring with birds kept under circumstances in which the presence of red mite is known to be quite out of the question. As a matter of fact the lines are due to temporary stoppages in the growth of the feather, probably caused by a chill, such as a serious drop in the normal temperature, or, with certain birds, to a cold bath, which temporarily checks the growth of the feathers.

TONING DOWN THE LIGHT.

When the moult has progressed until some portion of the new plumage is expected to put in an appearance, very soon it will become necessary to shut out some of the light. This will be in from two to three weeks after the birds have begun to drop their feathers freely. It is not by any means necessary to make the room or cages dark, as is sometimes imagined, and in the case of birds that are not being colour-fed they may be allowed the benefit of the full natural light if the owner cares to sacrifice a certain amount of tone of colour.

For the general stock it will suffice to merely subdue the light by keeping coloured blinds yellow, orange, or red for preference—hung before the windows. The use of Venetian blinds where available would be quite a good substitute. This will tone down the light all over the room.

But it will still be advisable to hang a curtain of some light material before the cages containing the most valuable birds. The cheapest kind of unbleached calico serves the purpose admirably, and is to be preferred to the plan of covering the cages with sheets of brown paper, which are apt to admit either too much or too little light into the cages. It will be a great convenience to have a curtain made to run on a tape and cover the whole stack of cages; suspend it about two or three inches away from the cage fronts. This method will admit sufficient light for the birds to find their way about the cages and to eat and drink; will allow free ventilation of the cages, and thus avoid stuffiness; and the cover may be instantly drawn across to one end, to leave the cages completely exposed for an hour or so morning and evening, whilst the birds are being fed and tended.

FURTHER HINTS.

A few grains of linseed may be given to each bird twice a week from the time they are ready to go into the moulting cages, as it will help to add a nice lustre and finish to the new plumage. The practice of giving sulphate of iron, or iron in some form, though serving a useful purpose in fixing the colour and making it more permanent, must not be commenced too early. Let the birds get well beyond the middle of the moult (as already pointed out in dealing with the colour-feeding portion of the process), and always see that iron is followed by some simple aperient.

When the moult is quite finished it is a good plan to again go over the cream of the stock and select all those which have come out good enough to warrant their appearance on the show bench, and cage them separately in perfectly clean cages, covered with some light flimsy material to exclude dirt and dust. By this means the birds may make one, two, or even three appearances in public before going through the ordeal of washing, and will doubtless gain in other ways, as it is only the most accomplished performers that can hope to wash a bird without some loss of the natural tone and bloom of the feathers.

CHAPTER XVIII

TRAINING FOR SHOW

If the first few words under this heading appear foreign to the subject we must crave the reader's indulgence. But having traced the career of the young birds step by step through the, colour-feeding and moulting processes, we would not leave the subject without mentioning one little item of some importance which may easily be forgotten by the novice. When we cautioned the reader not to take the birds off the colour-food too early, we should have gone on to say that every bird which finishes up with a nice even depth of colour and is likely to prove useful for show should continue to have a little colour-food at least once, or better still, twice a week all through the show season.

The object of this is two-fold: firstly, it helps to preserve the depth of tone, which, without this aid, is apt to begin to show a faded or washed-out appearance after a few weeks' wear; and, secondly, there is always a risk of stray feathers being lost accidently in the course of the show season, and if no colour-food had been given for some weeks these feathers would be

146

reproduced in their natural colour and give the bird a more or less patchy appearance, according to the number of feathers thus lost and reproduced.

Training the birds for show is part of the routine work of the experienced breeder. It may really be said to have neither beginning nor end, as it goes on continually all through the year, and falls in naturally between all kinds of bird room occupations. In short, the enthusiastic fancier—which not infrequently means the successful fancier—will utilise his spare hours and odd moments at any season in putting such birds as are at liberty for the purpose "through their paces" in the show cage. The aim and purpose of training is to teach each bird to pose itself in that position which is most typical of the breed it represents, and to show off its good points to the greatest advantage when in a show cage. And it should be made as perfect as possible in this art before being exhibited, so that it learns to know, in a way, what is required of it when one approaches its cage with a judging-stick to examine it critically, and assumes at once its typical pose. To attain this end requires much skill and patient plodding work, particularly with the young birds of the year. But it is work that is absolutely essential to success on the show bench, as one must easily understand when one reflects that a judge at a show probably has some scores, if not hundreds, of birds to deal with in a few hours, and consequently it is impossible for him to spend perhaps half an hour over a single bird that flutters wildly about its cage and stubbornly refuses to show its points. A bird of this type has to possess some superlative quality to obtain any recognition at all, and even in the rare cases when it does get noticed by reason of some obvious merits, it often has to give place to a less typical specimen that is better trained in the art of showing off what merit it does possess.

It is only possible to deal with the subject in general terms in these brief notes. In the first place, one must acquire a thorough knowledge of the good and bad points and the typical position of the breed one has to deal with. This cannot be better obtained than by close and careful study of the standard of perfection for the breed. These standards being all grouped together in *Cage Birds Annual,* may be easily referred to at any time.

Being now equipped for the task, the next thing is to get the bird tame and steady when placed in the show-cage. Each bird must be treated individually, and a part of its first few lessons must be to teach it to run from one cage to another in order to avoid handling it as far as possible. A slender twig or thin cane, long enough to reach easily to the back of the largest cage, is useful to keep at hand, and its frequent use helps to make the birds understand what is required of them when a judge approaches their cages with a judging-stick in hand. Take the show cage in one hand, open the door wide, then open wide the door of the cage containing the bird, place the two doorways close together, and with the cane in the other hand gently drive the bird through into the show-cage, and slip your hand between the two cages over the doorways whilst the doors are being safely closed again. It will require time and patience at the beginning, but after a few lessons the birds will soon learn to run from one cage to another when the doorways are placed together.

IN THE SHOW CAGE.

Having got the bird in a show-cage, place it alone on a table, or some convenient place, and leave it for a short time, until it is accustomed to its new surroundings. Then take your patience in both hands, and use all the arts and wiles in your power to get the bird to stand quite steady in its typical position for a few moments. Touch the wires gently with the end of the cane; take hold of the cage at the base and gently lift it up a little; tap the sides, or gently scratch the bottom; in short, do quite what the circumstances and the individual seem to require to bring about your object in getting the bird tame and steady, and to pose itself in the position required by the standard for its breed, so as to show all its good points to the best advantage when it is required to do so.

Do not expect too much at first. Remember that with young birds training it is apt to prove a trying and tedious task before the birds seem to get the least idea what is required of them. But after a time patience and perseverance always win, and progress is then much more rapid, and the advantage which a well-trained bird always gets on the show-bench will far outweigh all the time and labour bestowed upon its education. Therefore, during a bird's first season, at least, train much and train frequently, but always with the utmost patience and gentleness. Never lose your temper with a wild or dull bird; if you cannot avoid this, leave the bird in the show-cage for an hour or so and go away and "work off steam" elsewhere. Then you can go back and try again.

When you have finished each lesson give the bird some little dainty—a pinch of maw. or hemp, or niga, or a small piece of bread dipped in cold milk, or a scrap of some choice green food—and leave it in the show-cage for an hour or two In this way it soon feels quite at home in a show-cage, and gradually gets to associate it with its own abilities for "showing off."

FINAL POINTS.

There are but few other points we need dwell upon here Chief among these is one very important "don't." This is, never place your hand upon the top of the cage in which you are training a bird. Nothing is more likely to make a bird crouch across the perch, and as crouching is a serious fault in every variety, and a fatal blemisk in some breeds, it goes without saying that everything which is likely to give rise to the habit must be strictly avoided. In lifting or moving the cage about always take hold of it at the lower part near the base.

Our next and last point has a still more definite bearing upon training. Many devices have from time to time been made use of to assist in giving style to varieties known as "birds of position," such as suspending a piece of string or green food from the roof of the store or flight cages containing Yorkshires just over the perches, and at such a height that the birds have to stretch their bodies to get at it. It was believed, perhaps correctly, that by this means the birds acquired a more bold and upright carriage, which is one of their most valued points. A similar idea is embodied in the type of cage, which, we believe, is known among Yorkshire breeders as "peeping cages" or "peeping Tommies." These are two compartment cages, in which about a fifth part of the partition at the top is cut out and filled in with wires, the lower portion being left solid so as to obstruct the view from one compartment to the other, except by looking through the wires in the top part of the partition.

The height at which the wires begin is regulated by the height of the uppermost perches, and should be just enough to allow the birds, when standing quite upright on the upper perches and craning their necks, to see over the solid portion into the next compartment. When birds are confined in both compartments, they hear each other, and their natural curiosity impels them to be frequently stretching themselves as upright as possible in order to obtain a glimpse of their companions in the other compartment.

These cages, or rather, very good substitutes, may be easily made out of double breeding cages, either by having suitable movable partitions made to take the place of the ordinary partition, or by blocking up part of the ordinary partition with stout card-board, or some strong brown paper, to a sufficient height. That the theory is an excellent one cannot be gainsaid; whether the result in actual practice is to materially improve the style and carriage of the birds, we prefer to leave the individual fancier to discover, and with the earnest hope that it may be the crowning part of the beginner's first year of success, close these notes on the first steps in Canary breeding.

Printed in Great Britain
by Amazon